W9-AAE-329

THE IMPORTANCE OF

Neil Armstrong

These and other titles are included in The Importance Of biography series:

Maya Angelou
Louis Armstrong
Neil Armstrong
James Baldwin
Lucille Ball
The Beatles
Alexander Graham Bell
Napoleon Bonaparte
Julius Caesar
Rachel Carson
Fidel Castro
Charlie Chaplin
Charlemagne
Winston Churchill
Hillary Rodham Clinton
Christopher Columbus
Leonardo da Vinci
James Dean
Charles Dickens
Walt Disney
Dr. Seuss
F. Scott Fitzgerald
Henry Ford
Anne Frank
Benjamin Franklin
Mohandas Gandhi
John Glenn
Jane Goodall
Martha Graham
Lorraine Hansberry
Ernest Hemingway

Adolf Hitler
Thomas Jefferson
John F. Kennedy
Martin Luther King Jr.
Bruce Lee
Lenin
John Lennon
Abraham Lincoln
Charles Lindbergh
Douglas MacArthur
Paul McCartney
Margaret Mead
Golda Meir
Mother Teresa
Muhammad
John Muir
Richard M. Nixon
Pablo Picasso
Edgar Allan Poe
Queen Elizabeth I
Franklin D. Roosevelt
Jonas Salk
Margaret Sanger
William Shakespeare
Frank Sinatra
Tecumseh
J.R.R. Tolkien
Simon Wiesenthal
The Wright Brothers
Chuck Yeager

THE IMPORTANCE OF

Neil Armstrong

by Andrew A. Kling

LUCENT
BOOKS ®

THOMSON
━━━★━━━ ™
GALE

San Diego • Detroit • New York • San Francisco • Cleveland • New Haven, Conn. • Waterville, Maine • London • Munich

THOMSON
————————✷————————™
GALE

© 2004 by Lucent Books. Lucent Books is an imprint of The Gale Group, Inc.,
a division of Thomson Learning, Inc.

Lucent Books® and Thomson Learning™ are trademarks used herein under license.

For more information, contact
Lucent Books
27500 Drake Rd.
Farmington Hills, MI 48331-3535
Or you can visit our Internet site at http://www.gale.com

LIBRARY OF CONGRESS CATALOGING-IN-PUBLICATION DATA

Kling, Andrew A., 1961–
  Neil Armstrong / by Andrew A. Kling.
    p. cm. — (The importance of)
Summary: A biography of the first man on the moon, covering his life and his career
as an astronaut.
Includes bibliographical references and index.
  ISBN 1-59018-309-6 (hardback : alk. paper)
  1. Armstrong, Neil, 1930—Juvenile literature. 2. Astronauts—United States—Biography—
Juvenile literature. 3. Project Apollo (U.S.)—Juvenile literature. 4. Space flight to the
moon—Juvenile literature. [1. Armstrong, Neil, 1930– 2. Astronauts. 3. Project Apollo (U.S.)]
I. Title. II. Series.
  TL789.85.A75K58 2004
  629.45'0092—dc21
                                                                                  2003006257

Printed in the United States of America

Contents

Foreword

THE IMPORTANCE OF biography series deals with individuals who have made a unique contribution to history. The editors of the series have deliberately chosen to cast a wide net and include people from all fields of endeavor. Individuals from politics, music, art, literature, philosophy, science, sports, and religion are all represented. In addition, the editors did not restrict the series to individuals whose accomplishments have helped change the course of history. Of necessity, this criterion would have eliminated many whose contribution was great, though limited. Charles Darwin, for example, was responsible for radically altering the scientific view of the natural history of the world. His achievements continue to impact the study of science today. Others, such as Chief Joseph of the Nez Percé, played a pivotal role in the history of their own people. While Joseph's influence does not extend much beyond the Nez Percé, his nonviolent resistance to white expansion and his continuing role in protecting his tribe and his homeland remain an inspiration to all.

These biographies are more than factual chronicles. Each volume attempts to emphasize an individual's contributions both in his or her own time and for posterity. For example, the voyages of Christopher Columbus opened the way to European colonization of the New World. Unquestionably, his encounter with the New World brought monumental changes to both Europe and the Americas in his day. Today, however, the broader impact of Columbus's voyages is being critically scrutinized. *Christopher Columbus,* as well as every biography in The Importance Of series, includes and evaluates the most recent scholarship available on each subject.

Each author includes a wide variety of primary and secondary source quotations to document and substantiate his or her work. All quotes are footnoted to show readers exactly how and where biographers derive their information, as well as provide stepping stones to further research. These quotations enliven the text by giving readers eyewitness views of the life and times of each individual covered in The Importance Of series.

Finally, each volume is enhanced by photographs, bibliographies, chronologies, and comprehensive indexes. For both the casual reader and the student engaged in research, The Importance Of biographies will be a fascinating adventure into the lives of people who have helped shape humanity's past and present, and who will continue to shape its future.

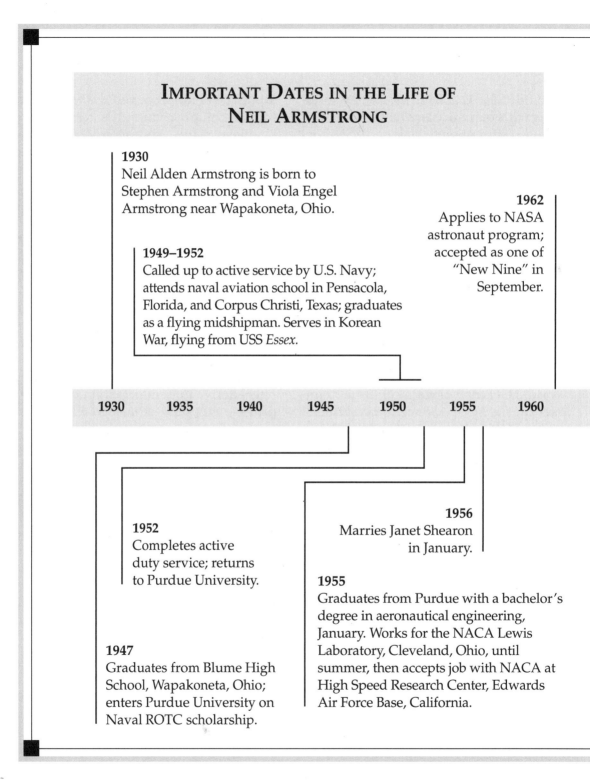

Important Dates in the Life of Neil Armstrong

1930
Neil Alden Armstrong is born to Stephen Armstrong and Viola Engel Armstrong near Wapakoneta, Ohio.

1949–1952
Called up to active service by U.S. Navy; attends naval aviation school in Pensacola, Florida, and Corpus Christi, Texas; graduates as a flying midshipman. Serves in Korean War, flying from USS *Essex*.

1962
Applies to NASA astronaut program; accepted as one of "New Nine" in September.

1930	1935	1940	1945	1950	1955	1960

1952
Completes active duty service; returns to Purdue University.

1956
Marries Janet Shearon in January.

1955
Graduates from Purdue with a bachelor's degree in aeronautical engineering, January. Works for the NACA Lewis Laboratory, Cleveland, Ohio, until summer, then accepts job with NACA at High Speed Research Center, Edwards Air Force Base, California.

1947
Graduates from Blume High School, Wapakoneta, Ohio; enters Purdue University on Naval ROTC scholarship.

1965
Serves as backup commander to *Gemini V* flight.

1980
Resigns from University of Cincinnati.

1966
Flies as commander of *Gemini VIII* flight, with Dave Scott as pilot.

1986
Serves as member of Rogers Board investigating space shuttle *Challenger* explosion.

1968
Named as backup commander for *Apollo 8*.

1989
Becomes chairman of AIL Systems.

1965   1970   1975   1980   1985   1990   1995

1994
Divorces Jan Armstrong; marries Carol Knight.

1971
Resigns from NASA; accepts professorship at University of Cincinnati. Buys farm in Lebanon, Ohio.

2000
AIL merges with EDO Corporation; Armstrong named chairman of EDO.

1969
Named commander of *Apollo 11*, January. Becomes first man to walk on the Moon, July 20. Appointed to Aeronautics Office, Washington, D.C.

2002
Retires as chairman of the board of EDO Corporation.

Apollo 11, July 20, 1969

On July 20, 1969, as millions of people around the world watched on television or listened in on radio, *Apollo 11*'s lunar module approached the surface of the Moon. While the mission's command module, piloted by Michael Collins, orbited the Moon, the smaller lunar module descended toward the lunar terrain. Inside the small spacecraft stood two American astronauts who had made the quarter-million-mile journey from Earth to attempt this first-ever lunar landing. Lunar module pilot Edwin "Buzz"

Neil Armstrong made history in 1969 when he became the first human to walk on the Moon.

Aldrin stood on the right side; *Apollo 11* commander Neil Armstrong stood on the left side. As Aldrin called out readings from the craft's computer, Armstrong guided the lunar module ever closer to the surface.

Armstrong's years of training and preparation and his flying expertise were now on display for the world to see. The computer on board, primitive by current standards, was overloaded by the complexities of the landing approach; Armstrong coolly took over the controls. He said later that the landing program "was taking us right into a football-[field–]sized crater, with a large number of boulders and rocks."[1]

With only seconds of rocket fuel left, Armstrong guided the lunar module above the Moon's surface and selected a suitable landing spot. At 4:17 P.M. eastern time, Armstrong and Aldrin gently touched down on the lunar surface, completing one of the most remarkable journeys in the history of humankind.

After checking the condition of the spacecraft, completing several chores, and resting briefly, Armstrong and Aldrin climbed into their spacesuits. More than six hours after they had landed, Armstrong opened the hatch and climbed down the ladder. When he set foot on the lunar surface, he became the first human being to take steps on another world. Aldrin joined him shortly thereafter. For approximately the next three hours, the astronauts completed experiments, tested the limits of their spacesuits, and took time to admire the lunar surface. Aldrin commented that the moon's dusty surface had turned his boots almost the color of cocoa; Armstrong noted that the soil was like "powdered charcoal."[2]

Many called this achievement a miracle of modern science. Richard M. Nixon, then president of the United States, hailed the week of *Apollo 11*'s mission as "the greatest week in the history of the world,"[3] and famed aviator Charles Lindbergh, in a letter to command module pilot Collins, exclaimed, "What a fantastic experience it must have been!"[4] Yet for thirty-eight-year-old *Apollo 11* commander Neil Alden Armstrong, this flight had been just one in a series of many flights dating back to his early childhood. His dreams of flying had led him around the world and now, in 1969, to the Moon. The *Apollo 11* flight had no doubt been an important milestone in Armstrong's life, but his life has included many more achievements and accomplishments. The importance of Neil Armstrong's life to history reaches far beyond that one breathtaking week in 1969.

Chapter

1 Dreams of Flight

Neil Armstrong is perhaps the most famous American astronaut, yet he is perhaps also the least well known. Some astronauts have sought the spotlight during and after their time in space; others have taken advantage of their name recognition to pursue jobs in private business, seek elected office, or endorse commercial products or personal causes. Neil Armstrong, on the other hand, is an intensely private man whose dreams of flight brought him into the spotlight at a time when his particular expertise was needed; once the mission for which he was hired had ended, he was content to move on. In the years since his achievements as a part of the manned space program, which culminated when he became the first man to set foot on the Moon, he has striven to remain out of the public eye, carefully choosing when and where to attend gatherings or commemorations.

Yet although some see this behavior as standoffish or even snobbish, others who know him well understand that this quiet and reserved demeanor has been a part of Armstrong's character ever since childhood.

EARLY DAYS

Neil Alden Armstrong was born on August 5, 1930, in the living room of his grandparents' home near Wapakoneta, Ohio, in Auglaize County. Located in the western part of Ohio, the county was home in the 1930s to roughly twenty-eight thousand Americans, many of whom were descendants of early settlers and more recent German, Scots, and Irish immigrants. Wapakoneta, the county seat, had about seven thousand residents, and according to one author, was "a place whose open manners, tree-lined streets and abundance of old-fashioned two-story clapboard houses made it almost a model of small-town mid-America."[5] The farm was much like many others in the county, with crops of wheat, corn, or soybeans and livestock such as cattle or hogs. It belonged to his mother's parents, the Engels, whose daughter, Viola, had married Stephen Armstrong. Neil was Stephen and Viola's first child.

Neil's parents were, in his words many years later, "characteristic of the area where I grew up. . . . It was my observation that the people of that community felt it was important to do a useful job and do it well."[6] While Viola maintained the household that eventually included a daughter named June and another son, named Dean, Stephen Armstrong worked for the state of Ohio as an auditor of county records.

As an auditor, Stephen Armstrong was responsible for studying the financial records of counties across Ohio. He scrutinized them, ensuring that the record-

Although Armstrong is the most famous American astronaut, he prefers to keep his private life private.

keeping methods were accurate and complete. At the same time, he stayed alert for anything that seemed out of the ordinary. This included oversights (such as an expense inadvertently left out of the records), errors (such as an expense for the schools department entered in the records of the parks department), or even examples of wrongdoing. His scrupulous attention to detail resulted in several cheating officials' going to jail, but Stephen's work required him to move the family several times during the first six years of Neil's life, to be in the county he was auditing.

During these years, the United States was in the midst of the Great Depression; money was always tight. Neil recalled, "We were not deprived, but there was never a great deal of money around. On that score we had it no worse and no better than thousands of other families,"[7] so the Armstrongs traveled light, living in small apartments during their frequent moves from town to town throughout Ohio.

During these years, his parents did their best to keep a nurturing environment for their children. Neil's mother spent hours reading to him, and he began to talk very early in life. He developed into a bright and curious boy who loved reading. He had read over one hundred children's books during first grade and skipped a grade one year when his family moved.

But the family's frequent moves made it difficult for Neil to make and keep friends. His mother later calculated that she and her husband had moved the family sixteen times, and it was always a challenge to make friends in a new environment as Stephen's job brought them to a new town.

Neil developed a quiet and reserved demeanor that led many to describe him as shy. Before the age of thirteen he had attended schools in the Ohio towns of Warren, Jefferson, Moulton, St. Mary's, and Upper Sandusky. Although he recalled having friendships in every school, he did not make any lifelong friends until he reached middle school. But it was during these early years that Neil began a fascination with flight.

BOYHOOD DREAMS OF FLIGHT

The young Neil Armstrong was not alone in his interest in flight. The 1930s in the United States were a fantastic time for flying enthusiasts. Barely twenty-five years had passed since the Wright brothers had flown their first airplane in a powered and controlled flight. Yet by the time Neil was born, aviators such as Charles Lindbergh had crossed the Atlantic Ocean nonstop, and the United States Army had sent a group of airplanes on a multistop flight around the world. Flying was becoming more popular as new developments in engines and airplane designs were leading to safer, faster, and more maneuverable aircraft. Additionally, competitions were held across the country and around the world to challenge aviators and designers to break distance and speed records. One of the most famous of these competitions was held in Neil's home state.

The Cleveland Air Races were home to daring feats of aviation. Pilots raced around closed courses to achieve glory as the fastest and most skilled flyers, and the races often concluded with participants flying cross-country to arrive at Cleveland's airfield. Spectators at the races over the years witnessed flights by aviators whose names have become legendary in the history of aviation, including Roscoe Turner, Amelia Earhart, Jimmy Doolittle, and Jackie Cochran.

When Neil was just two years old, his father took him to the Cleveland Air Races.

THE JOY OF READING

Neil Armstrong's mother, Viola, instilled in her son the joy of reading. But unlike many youngsters, his tastes did not run to comic book or science fiction adventure. In a 2001 interview as part of the NASA Johnson Space Center Oral History Project, Armstrong recalled:

I was an avid reader—and I read all kinds of things. I spent a lot of time in the library and took a lot of books out of the library, both fiction and non-fiction. However, when I was building things, like models and so on, they were predominantly focused on aviation related "stuff." . . . I recall that I read a lot of the aviation magazines of the time, *Flight* and *Air Trails* and *Model Airplane News,* and anything I could get my hands on.

The youngster delighted in watching the speeding and swooping aircraft.

Neil took his first ride in an airplane just four years later. Stephen Armstrong understood his son's interest in flying but could not afford to pay for a ride. He then discovered that an airfield not far from where they were living offered discounted airplane rides on Sundays. When they took a flight in a Ford Tri-Motor airplane, Stephen said, Neil found it exhilarating: "Neil enjoyed it tremendously, but I was scared."[8]

That airplane ride and his visits to the air races helped frame Neil's boyhood dreams of flight. By the time he was in elementary school, he had decided he wanted to be an aircraft designer. He started building small wooden models of airplanes he had seen or read about in books and magazines. He earned extra money for more models by taking part-time jobs as the family continued moving throughout the state. He later remembered that his studies of airplanes filled notebooks with "scraps of information about makes of aircraft, specifications, and performances."[9] He also built his own miniature wind tunnel while he was in high school to test how well his models would fly. He wanted to be able to vary the speed of the fan generating the wind to simulate how his models would fly in different conditions and at different wind speeds. All this would tell him how they would perform at varying flying speeds. However, the wind tunnel experiment was not entirely successful. He recalled that his efforts "blew out a lot of fuses in my home."[10]

The Armstrongs' travels across Ohio ended when Stephen got a new job with the state of Ohio's Department of Public Wel-

Armstrong's lifelong fascination with flight began with a visit to the Cleveland Air Races where aviators like Amelia Earhart (pictured) competed.

fare. The family bought a house in Wapakoneta in 1943, the year after Neil entered high school. Now that the family was settling down, Neil discovered that his dreams of flight could extend beyond his collection of model airplanes. With the prospect of his family living in Wapakoneta for the foreseeable future, Neil realized that he could

YOUTHFUL ACTIVITIES

In many ways, Neil Armstrong's teenage years were very similar to those of other youngsters across the country in the 1930s. Correspondent William K. Stevens wrote about Neil's nonaviation diversions in his article "The Crew: What Kind of Men Are They?":

Aside from his aeronautics, the young Neil filled his time with Boy Scout activities, reading, playing baritone horn in the school band and for a jazz combo he organized, [and] learning the piano. . . . For all of his shyness and apparent immaturity, the teenage Neil went about his activities with an inner drive and quiet decisiveness that impressed his friends and earned him this descriptive line in the Blume High yearbook: "He thinks, he acts, 'tis done."

undertake a project that might take several years to complete without having it interrupted or ended unsuccessfully by another family move. After visiting the airfield near Wapakoneta and talking to the people who worked there, he discovered that he could take lessons to learn how to become a pilot.

LEARNING TO FLY

Neil looked upon getting his pilot's license as a way to design better airplanes. He felt that a good designer ought to understand how an airplane operated, but flying lessons cost nine dollars an hour, far more than he could afford. So Neil started saving his money. He took a sequence of part-time jobs, including working in a bakery, a drugstore, a hardware store, a grocery store, and at the Wapakoneta airfield washing airplanes. By the time he was fifteen, he began taking lessons, scheduling each as soon as he could afford it and was not attending school or working. Then he would hitch-

hike the three miles out of town to the airfield to continue his flight training.

Three local pilots, Aubrey Knudegard, Frank Lucia, and Charlie Finkbine, gave Neil his first lessons in an airplane built by the Aeronca Company called the *Champion.* The *Champion* was similar to many other airplanes of its day. It was a single-engine airplane with a cloth-covered metal-tube frame. The high-mounted wings were also cloth covered, with a wood-frame interior. It measured twenty-one feet from propeller to tail, and its wings were thirty-five feet long. Weighing only 750 pounds empty, the *Champion's* small size and light weight made it ideal for grass fields like Wapakoneta's, as it did not require a large hangar or many people to move it around with the engine off. The sixty-five horsepower engine brought the *Champion* to a top speed of one hundred miles per hour, which was not particularly fast even in the 1940s.

But the *Champion* also seated two, enabling an instructor and a student pilot to sit inside the cockpit during lessons. The student sat at the controls while the instructor sat in the seat behind the student, watching everything the student did and offering advice and instruction as the student learned to fly.

As a student pilot in Wapakoneta, Neil progressed quickly. Within months, he had completed the requirements for earning his pilot's license, but by law he had to wait until he turned sixteen to receive his student-pilot license. On Neil's sixteenth birthday, he passed his certification by making his first solo flight from the grass airfield in Wapakoneta.

It was a very exciting time for Neil, who was one of just three in a class of about thirty-five teenage boys who earned his license at that time. But never one to brag about his accomplishments, he told few of his classmates that they had a pilot in their midst. Additionally, Neil was still quiet and reserved, and he had few close friends with whom he could share this significant achievement. But this achievement and his love of flying would soon take him away from Wapakoneta.

THE WORLD OUTSIDE

Neil certainly knew that there was more to the world than Wapakoneta, Ohio. When he entered the town's Blume High School in the fall of 1943, the United States was fighting World War II. The U.S. armed forces were fighting the Germans in Italy and the Japanese in the Pacific Ocean. The defeat of Germany and Japan seemed a long way off, and many of the young men attending classes with Neil knew that they would enlist in the armed services once they had graduated from high school. However, the war ended in August 1945, between Neil's sophomore and junior years. Suddenly, young men who had been planning to go to war were faced with making new decisions about their future.

Armstrong learned to fly when he was fifteen years old and was certain he wanted to pursue a career in aviation.

Neil Armstrong was no different. He was certain he wanted to enter the field of aviation, possibly as an aeronautical engineer or aircraft designer, but that would mean continuing his education by going to college. He knew that his family had little money for that purpose, so he began looking into scholarship programs. One program that seemed promising came from the U.S. Navy.

DREAMS OF COLLEGE

The navy's Naval Reserve Officer Training Corps (NROTC) offered a program called the Holloway Plan. The plan appealed to Neil because it offered recipients a way to pay most of the expenses of a college education. If he was lucky enough to be chosen for this program, he would be able to accomplish his dream: to attend college on scholarship immediately after high school and study aeronautical engineering.

But before Neil could think about applying for college, he had to apply for the Holloway Plan. The nationwide program was extremely competitive and required a qualifications exam. Shortly before graduation from high school, Neil took the challenging all-day test. Years later, he said that although he could not remember the details of the test, "I'm sure [it] had a focus on things that would be appropriate to aviation, because it was an aviation-directed program."[11]

Later that spring, he was notified that the navy was offering him a scholarship associated with the NROTC under the Holloway Plan. In exchange for three years of active duty with the navy, including a year of aviation training, the U.S. government would pay his college expenses, plus a small stipend (or monthly salary) for living expenses. According to authors Gene Farmer and Dora Jane Hamblin,

> One day in 1947 the letter arrived: he had been accepted. Neil's mother remembered the day only too well: "I was in the basement getting out quart jars of canned fruit to bake some pies. He called so loudly, 'Mom, Mom,' that he scared me to death. I dropped a jar of blackberries on my big toe. I must have broken the toe—it was black and blue for weeks. But that was such a great day."[12]

Accepting a scholarship in the Holloway Plan was a seven-year commitment. Those who participated in the program were expected to attend two years of college before their active duty, followed by three years of active duty and two years of college studies. However, as the participants would become members of the NROTC, they were subject to military orders. The navy informed them that they could be called to active duty at any time at the navy's discretion during those first two years of college. Neil was not interested in a military career, but he felt that the scholarship might offer the only way to get to college.

With the Holloway Plan set to pay his college expenses, Neil and his family started investigating colleges with aeronautical engineering programs. At the recommendation of a high school instructor, they looked into the program at Purdue

THE HOLLOWAY PLAN

Neil Armstrong was one of a select few who were able to take advantage of the NROTC scholarship program in the late 1940s. According to the website of the Flying Midshipmen Association:

The Holloway Aviation Midshipmen Program began in 1946 and gathered in all of the Aviation Cadets, USNR [Unites States Naval Reserve], in the U.S. Navy's pilot training pipeline [that] could be convinced or wanted to become Regular Navy. The program was named for Rear Admiral James L. Holloway Jr. . . . who had been chartered to design an overall acquisition and retention plan for building the post–World War II Officer Corps of the Navy. The incentive of a college education was offered as well to high school seniors as motivation to sign up for Navy flight training.

The program lasted for only 3 years; the last Aviation Midshipman was in pre-flight class 1949 (he got his "gold wings" in 1951). During this time, there were [approximately] 3000 fledgling "fly-boys" who had the rank of Aviation Midshipman, USN. One of the major reasons the program had to be terminated was the inability of the Navy to honor promises made as inducements to join. Also contributing to the cancellation of the program in 1949 was a push at top civilian government levels to do away with Naval Aviation as a separate entity and have one combined Air Force. The start of the Korean War in June 1950 put a halt to that effort. Hundreds of Aviation Midshipmen . . . flew off carriers and in other maritime support roles; many were killed, others became prisoners of war. Graduates of the Aviation Midshipmen program participated in every major aviation event from the Berlin Airlift [in 1949] to the conflict in Vietnam; sixteen of their number eventually rose to flag rank.

University in nearby West Lafayette, Indiana, and Neil chose to apply for it. In the fall of 1947, Neil enrolled at Purdue. When the school year started that September, he was just one month past his seventeenth birthday. He was leaving home for the first time and was facing the prospect of living and making friends in a new environment. His brother, Dean, remembered many years later that when Neil left for Purdue, he was still a teen who had not yet reached his adult height. But the next several years presented numerous challenges that helped Neil Armstrong mature from a quiet, reserved, and immature teen into a quiet, reserved, and confident man.

2 The Flying Midshipman

When Neil Armstrong arrived at Purdue University in the fall of 1947, he found himself quite literally a boy among men. Not only was he at least a year younger than the average college freshman, he was also much younger than some of the other students on campus whose education had been deferred or interrupted by World War II.

Across the United States, thousands of discharged veterans were taking advantage of the GI bill to continue or finish their education. The GI bill was a U.S. government program that made a college education much less expensive for these veterans than for regular students. Because of this, college enrollments skyrocketed. At Purdue in the fall of 1947, over seven hundred students were enrolled in the aeronautical engineering program alone. (By contrast, the program regularly has fewer than three hundred today.)

Unlike the many veterans around him in the classrooms of Purdue, Armstrong's military service was still ahead of him. The Holloway Plan was paying for his education, which meant that he was part of the Naval Reserve Officer Training Corps (NROTC), but his three years of active duty might be as much as two years away. Until that time came, Armstrong threw himself into the aeronautical engineering curriculum.

AERONAUTICAL ENGINEERING AT PURDUE

Purdue's aeronautical engineering program has a rich history that started in the early 1920s, and by 1941 the university expanded its aeronautical engineering curriculum to a full four-year program. Neil Armstrong joined this program when he enrolled at Purdue in 1947. He knew that the world of aviation was changing rapidly, and he wanted to be part of this challenging field.

World War II had brought tremendous advancements in aeronautical engineering. Perhaps the most conspicuous of these achievements was the jet aircraft. Jet engines had been invented before the war began and had seen some limited use during the war. But immediately following the war, they came to the forefront of the experimental fields of aeronautics. In fact, in the fall of 1947, U.S. Air Force pilot Charles E. ("Chuck") Yeager, flying an experimental jet airplane called the *X-1*, flew faster than the speed of sound, breaking the so-called sound barrier.

For flying enthusiasts such as Armstrong and his classmates, this was an event of great interest. Some in the field of aviation said flying faster than the speed of sound was impossible because many aircraft had broken apart from the stresses associated with these high speeds. Armstrong's own flying had been limited to single-engine, propeller-driven aircraft from the grass airfield outside of Wapakoneta; the Aeronca *Champion*'s top speed was only one hundred miles an hour. Now Yeager, flying 662 miles per hour, had demonstrated that constructing an engine to propel an airplane faster than the speed of sound was possible, as was constructing an aircraft sturdy enough to withstand the tremendous air pressure forces that an airplane generates as it approaches and passes through the sound barrier.

In 1947, as Armstrong enrolled in Purdue University's aeronautical engineering program, U.S. Air Force pilot Chuck Yeager (pictured) made aviation history by flying faster than the speed of sound.

All aeronautical engineering students were familiar with air pressure forces. Armstrong understood that the key to aircraft design lies in understanding these forces, as well as understanding how they affect both a wing's ability to generate lift and an aircraft's maneuverability. His experiments with his model planes and his homemade wind tunnel had dealt with these same forces. But now Yeager's flight symbolized a new beginning in aeronautical engineering and the challenges of aircraft design and control that these supersonic flights presented.

At this time, Armstrong was not only following the latest advancements in aviation but was also immersed in the aeronautical engineering program in college. He had expected to complete two years at Purdue before being called to active service in the navy. But in the middle of his second year, the navy exercised its option and required him to begin his active duty immediately. He was notified to report to naval flight school in Pensacola, Florida. His education would now proceed in a different direction.

FLYING FOR HIS COUNTRY

For Armstrong and his fellow pilots, the navy's aviation training was divided into three parts. First was a four-month regimen

A TYPICAL POSTWAR AERONAUTICAL ENGINEERING CURRICULUM

Commercial and military aeronautical engineering was undergoing a revolution in the years after World War II. New materials, technologies, and philosophies of development and design that had been explored during the war were slow to be incorporated into college course offerings. The University of Minnesota's document "History of the Aeronautical Engineering Department at the University of Minnesota 1929–1962" illustrates this. This excerpt describes a typical curriculum in the postwar period; note the absence of references to the new field of jet propulsion.

The department offered eighteen courses during its first year [of the four-year aeronautical engineering curriculum in 1946]. [Professor John] Akerman taught the introductory courses in aviation and aircraft engines. These courses dealt primarily with hardware and pilot knowledge: structures, instruments, electrical systems, navigation, and communications. Charles Boehnlein continued as the professor for the more theoretical courses that dealt with aerodynamics. His three-course series introduced the concepts of aerodynamic forces, stability, propeller theory, and laboratory practices. Professor Joseph Wise from the civil engineering department taught two classes on structural stresses and forces as they apply to airframes and landing gear. One instructor, Mr. Hoglund, rounded out the faculty. Hoglund took responsibility for the laboratory courses, which covered airplane design, airplane parts and their construction and airships.

Fighter planes fly in formation above an aircraft carrier during World War II. In naval flight school, Armstrong learned how to fly in such formations and how to land on aircraft carriers.

of physical fitness training along with flight training called ground school. Ground school teaches prospective pilots the mechanics of flying, such as how to use aircraft equipment and engines, along with the basics of navigation, all before they fly aircraft. The navy called the second part basic training; it taught navy procedures for taking off, landing, navigating, flying cross-country, and flying using instruments only. Basic training also provided some techniques not taught to civilians, such as flying with other aircraft in military formations, learning how to drop bombs, and firing guns. Additionally, because this was a navy program, the pilots also learned how to land on aircraft carriers, practicing their landings on ships off the coast of Florida.

After basic training, the navy sent Armstrong and many of his fellow pilots to Corpus Christi, Texas, for the third and final part of their training, advanced training. Armstrong trained to fly the F8F *Bearcat*, a fighter aircraft. The *Bearcats* were single-seat, propeller-driven fighters that had been used during the last days of World War II. They were being replaced in active navy units at sea and abroad by jet aircraft, and the navy was using its remaining *Bearcats* for training. In this airplane, Armstrong learned advanced techniques of navigation over land and water and ways to use electronic aids to find the aircraft carrier at sea. He also learned the plane's offensive and defensive capabilities and received more training in carrier landings.

By August 1950, Armstrong had spent almost eighteen months in active duty training. He was now a fully qualified navy pilot. Because he was part of the NROTC, the navy considered him a naval officer in training, or a midshipman. The navy designated him and his colleagues as flying midshipmen, one with naval aviation training. In the slang of the service, he had "received his wings."

Additionally, Armstrong was in a very exclusive group. Because the Holloway Plan had sent them to specialized naval aviation training, and because the navy offered no more new scholarships after 1949, he was, as he recalled later, "one of those rare birds, a midshipman with wings."[13] But after roughly eighteen months of training, he still had another eighteen months to go in his three-year active duty requirement. However, world events meant he would be on active duty longer than that. All eyes were turned toward a new war on the Korean Peninsula.

SERVICE IN KOREA

Following World War II, the Korean Peninsula was divided into two countries: North Korea, which was run by a Communist government, and South Korea, which was governed by a more democratic system. On June 25, 1950, North Korean troops invaded South Korea, which began a war that lasted three years and involved over twenty countries from the United Nations, including the United States.

By the time Armstrong had finished his advanced training in August 1950, the war was two months old. U.S. Army and Navy forces had come to the aid of South Korea, and when his training ended, Armstrong requested an assignment to the navy's Pacific Fleet. By the end of 1950, he had been assigned to a jet aircraft fighter squadron designated VF-51.

Because they were headed to the war, the squadron's members received a great deal of additional training, including learning how to fly a new jet aircraft called the F9F *Panther.* This jet's top speed was over 150 miles an hour faster than that of the propeller-driven *Bearcat,* which meant that the *Panther* handled differently than the *Bearcat.* For example, it had different maneuvering capabilities, such as a faster rate of climb and a higher landing speed.

Before they could fly in combat, the pilots had to learn the *Panther*'s intricacies, as well as how to land it on their carrier, the USS *Essex.* They learned how to defend the navy ships from enemy air attacks and how to attack targets on land. At age twenty, Armstrong was learning to fly one of the navy's most advanced airplanes, and he was about to go into combat.

COMBAT IN THE AIR

Over the next two years, Armstrong flew aerial combat missions from the USS *Essex* off the east coast of the Korean Peninsula. His squadron had been trained in air-to-air combat, but, Armstrong recalled, "There were no enemy planes in our area. So our work was air-to-ground. Bridge breaking, train stopping, tank shooting and that sort of thing."[14] He flew a total of seventy-eight missions, and although Armstrong does not

OTHERS WERE NOT SO LUCKY

The soft-spoken Neil Armstrong is generally reluctant to discuss his active duty in the Korean War, but in First on the Moon: A Voyage with Neil Armstrong, Michael Collins, and Edwin E. Aldrin, Jr. *Gene Farmer and Dora Jane Hamblin show that aviation in wartime is a dangerous business:*

By the time Neil returned to the United States in the spring of 1952, a lot of faces were missing in his squadron. The official report on Squadron 51 had some somber lines in it: "3 September, 1951, Ensign Neil A. Armstrong bailed out of his F9F-2 aircraft, successfully using the ejection seat. 4 September, 1951, Lieutenant (junior grade) James J. Ashford, USN[avy], was killed . . . while on an armed reconnaissance flight . . . cause unknown. 4 September, 1951, Lieutenant (junior grade) Ross K. Bramwell, USN, was killed. . . . 16 September, 1951, F2H-2 Bureau No. 124968, VF-172, bounced over the barriers on landing and crashed into aircraft parked forward, bursting into flame. The following men were listed missing and presumed to be dead: Neifer, Earl K.; Barfield, Wade H.; and Harell, Charles L."

recall his first mission from the *Essex,* one particular mission stands out in his mind.

On September 3, 1951, Armstrong was flying his plane in the mountains of North Korea, acting as "wing man" to a U.S. Air Force major named John Carpenter; that is, he was flying close by Carpenter's plane to be able to provide support if necessary. As they flew through a valley, Armstrong's plane hit a cable strung between the two hills. He was traveling so fast that the cable sliced completely through the plane's right wing, and Armstrong lost about six or eight feet of the wing.

Armstrong and Carpenter discussed the emergency over the radio and agreed that trying to land the airplane in its damaged condition would probably be too dangerous. Losing that much of the wing meant the plane would be unstable at the low land-

ing speed, and the pilot could be injured or even killed as he tried to land. So with Carpenter alongside, Armstrong flew his damaged plane south until they were out of enemy territory. Near the U.S. Marines airfield at Pohang, South Korea, he ejected from the airplane and parachuted to safety.

This was Armstrong's first parachute jump. Although navy pilots always wore parachutes during missions, Armstrong's naval aviation training had not covered how to use them. One of his NROTC classmates, however, had received training in parachutes and had shared his knowledge with the other pilots. On September 3, Armstrong put that knowledge to good use. It may have saved his life.

When Armstrong landed, U.S. Marines working at the airfield met him and soon returned him to the *Essex* to continue flying.

Although he completed three years of required service while the *Essex* was still at sea, he decided to stay on active duty until the ship completed her assignment off the Korean Peninsula. In an interview many years later, he joked that he was faced with a choice at the end of the three years: He could either extend his tour or "swim home. So I extended."[15]

The extension meant Armstrong spent a few more months at sea in the spring of 1952. Meanwhile, he continued to think about the future. He had several options available: He could stay in the navy and make a career of active duty; he could use the skills the navy taught him in some civilian capacity, such as commercial aviation; or he could return to Purdue University to finish his education. After considering his options, he decided to make education the highest priority, so when he was discharged from the navy in 1952, he returned to Purdue.

FAMILIAR PLACES AND NEW FACES

Armstrong returned to Purdue's West Lafayette, Indiana, campus in the fall of 1952. When he arrived, he discovered that something unexpected had happened during the three-and-a-half years he had been away.

During high school and much of his time in the navy, Armstrong had been the youngest face in the crowd. Now, however, as a twenty-two-year-old student resuming his second year of college, it seemed that the other students were much younger than he was. The majority of the other students in their sophomore year were nineteen or twenty years old. Additionally, most of the World War II veterans who had populated the campus when Armstrong first enrolled at Purdue had graduated or moved on. Armstrong soon found that, because of his three years in the navy, he was both chronologically and psychologically older than his classmates.

He soon fell into a routine of hard work, both in and out of the classroom. He landed a job delivering the campus newspaper, and during his early morning rounds he repeatedly ran into another student named Janet Shearon. Jan had a passion for swimming and had many early morning laboratory classes, so she was also up early. They discovered that they shared an interest in airplanes; Jan's father, a physician in Illinois, had owned one for flying back and forth to the family's summer home in Wisconsin. And each saw in the other a similar interest in keeping busy and a devotion to learning. But characteristically, Armstrong was reserved in admitting his admiration for Jan and did not ask her for a date until two years later.

By then, it was late 1954, and Armstrong had nearly completed his requirements for graduation. He received a bachelor of science degree in aeronautical engineering in January 1955 and applied for a position with the National Advisory Council for Aeronautics (NACA) at Edwards Air Force Base in California. He didn't get it, but the NACA sent his application to its other laboratories, and the Lewis Flight Propulsion Laboratory in Cleveland, Ohio, offered him a job. He later remembered that it was "the lowest-paying job I was offered coming out of college,"[16] but he decided to take it nonetheless.

FLYING FOR HIS COUNTRY AGAIN

Armstrong moved to Cleveland in early 1955 and spent several months at the Lewis laboratory as a civilian research scientist, which was actually the dual role of test pilot and research engineer. One of his projects involved flying modified DC-3 airplanes over neighboring Lake Erie in search of bad weather. His team tested various experimental deicing techniques and equipment on the airplanes to determine which were the most efficient at shedding the dangerous accumulations of ice on the wings. Another project involved flying over the Atlantic Ocean and test-firing rockets to learn about how various types of metals from which the rockets were constructed performed under high stress. During this time, he continued to date Jan and to drive back and forth from Cleveland to Wapakoneta to see his family.

Armstrong met Janet Shearon at Purdue University in 1952, but he waited two years to ask her for a date.

Although his position had its rewards, as the months passed, Armstrong realized that the primary function of the NACA at Lewis was not examining experimental results or developing advancement in technology. Instead, publishing reports for the government and papers for publication in aeronautical journals seemed to be very important. Everything that laboratory staff prepared for publication had to undergo a rigorous examination by a review committee—not for content but for grammar and punctuation. Armstrong gained a respect for the committee's devotion to the elegance and nuances of the written language, but he wanted to fly and do more aeronautical engineering.

Fortunately, he didn't have to wait long for a new opportunity. In the summer of 1955, he received a job offer from Edwards Air Force Base. He said that he "thought about it all of fifteen seconds and agreed."[17] Not only was this a test pilot's job, a position for which he had originally applied, but he also felt that it would give him the chance to do the ex-perimental aircraft development, testing, and flying that he had not had during his time at Lewis. He prepared to move across the country to California. An exciting and challenging part of his life was about to begin.

But before he could move to Edwards, he needed to see Jan. He had proposed marriage to her that summer, and he went to see her in northern Wisconsin, where she was working as a summer camp counselor. Now he asked her to join him on the journey, but she was not going to rush into marriage. Years later, she teased her husband about his visit, joking that it seemed to her that the only reason he wanted her to join him on the trip was because he would get paid a higher mileage rate from the NACA for his move to California. She recalled, "He said that if I would marry him and come along in the car he'd get six cents a mile for the trip. If I didn't, he'd only get four."[18] But Jan gently declined, and Neil drove on to California alone to become the NACA's newest test pilot.

3 Challenges in the Air and on the Ground

In the summer of 1955, Neil Armstrong packed his belongings into his car, said good-bye to his family and to Jan, and drove across the country. His destination was Edwards Air Force Base in California and a new job with the National Advisory Council for Aeronautics (NACA) High Speed Flight Station. He was still a civilian employee of the NACA, although many of the other employees at Edwards were members of the military. He hoped that this job would allow him to put his aeronautical engineering skills to good use. The new job of test pilot and his new life in California both turned out to be filled with challenges.

FLYING AT EDWARDS

His first challenge was getting to know the work environment at Edwards Air Force Base. Encompassing several dry lake beds in the California desert northeast of Los Angeles, the base was the ideal location for flying experimental aircraft. According to author Andrew Chaikin,

> Edwards was a place of blast-furnace heat, howling winds, and utter desolation, but it was heaven on earth for

pilots. Dawn came still and clear, spilling over distant mountain ranges onto a smooth, hard expanse of clay that seemed as vast as the cloudless blue canopy above. . . . NACA's High Speed Flight Station was perched on the edge of Rogers Dry Lake. The NACA fliers epitomized a new breed of test pilot, engineers as much as aviators, that had emerged since the Second World War. Unlike the air force pilots at Edwards . . . the NACA pilots delved into lengthy, often tedious analyses that were the heart of test flight. The combination of meticulous research and all kinds of flying opportunities—both mundane and exotic—was what made Edwards a place to be cherished. [19]

When Armstrong joined the staff at Edwards in the summer of 1955, a number of "X projects" were under way in various stages of completion. In the world of aviation, the X designation denotes an experimental aircraft. Because aircraft development and design is a lengthy process, the X designation is often part of a development concept, called a project, for years before the aircraft is actually built.

Experimental aircraft on display at NACA High Speed Flight Station at Edwards Air Force Base in 1952. Armstrong became a civilian test pilot here in 1955.

One of these projects, called the X-15, was the reason that Armstrong was there in the first place. Government planners envisioned the X-15 project, designed to test both speed and altitude limits for airplanes, in 1952 and first formally proposed it to the NACA and the U.S. Air Force in 1954. Not long afterward, Armstrong was hired as a NACA pilot; his job eventually included testing for the X-15.

ENGINEERING, 1950S STYLE

The popular image of the job of test pilot only scratches the surface of the job's reality. Long before entering a new airplane's cockpit and attempting the craft's first flight, the pilot needs to understand the performance of the aircraft currently being tested, as well as that of the chase planes, the aircraft that accompany, observe, and monitor these tests.

But Armstrong's position for the NACA went far beyond actual flying. Many years later, he recalled that his role at Edwards involved a great deal more work on the ground than in the air. "Our principal responsibility was engineering work. We did not do a lot of flying. It was program development, devising simulations, looking at the problems of flight, and trying to figure out ways we could test those things and devise solutions to those problems."[20]

In the 1950s, developing new aircraft designs and devising simulations of these new aircraft in flight was painstaking work. Twenty-first-century aeronautical engineers use modern computer-assisted drawing programs to create aircraft configurations, computer-driven flight simulators to test multiple design schemes, as well as such now-everyday devices as electronic calculators to perform mathematical computations. But when Armstrong arrived at Edwards, computer technology was in its infancy. In the 1950s, engineers did a large part of their work with paper and pencils. They made calculations using instruments called slide rules, and engineers used mechanical drawing tools such as compasses, protractors and T-squares to produce renderings of every aspect of an aircraft's design, from the nose to the tail and from the landing gear to the cockpit canopy. It was meticulous and often repetitive work, as a small modification might require a completely new set of drawings. In the mid- and late 1950s, however, these extremely tedious, labor-intensive methods represented the only available technology, and Armstrong had to prove to the project

Armstrong operates a simulator for the X-15 rocket plane. Armstrong helped NACA to develop simulations for new aircraft designs.

leaders that he could master them as well as master their airplanes.

The project leaders at Edwards soon determined that Armstrong was a capable addition to their team. He became part of a team of engineers that, over the next several years, worked closely with a variety of government contractors around the country to make tremendous contributions to the field of aeronautics. By this time, his career was stable enough that he could contemplate not just his professional future, but his personal future as well. To him, that meant one person: Jan Shearon.

FAMILY LIFE

In January 1956, Neil Armstrong and Jan Shearon were married. When Jan came to California, the young couple looked for a home away from the base. At the time, most of the test pilots lived in the nearby town of Lancaster. The Armstrongs, however, chose to live in the foothills of the San Gabriel Mountains, about an hour's drive from the base. The house was a former forest ranger's cabin, with no electricity and no running water. When their first child, a son named Eric, was born in June 1957, the couple had renovated only to the extent of installing cold-water plumbing.

TRAGEDY STRIKES THE ARMSTRONG FAMILY

In early 1959, Jan Armstrong gave birth to the family's second child and first girl, whom the couple named Karen. However, in 1961, tragedy struck the family, as authors Farmer and Hamblin describe in their book First on the Moon:

In 1961, when some of Neil's work took him to Seattle [to work with an engineering firm contracted with Edwards], the family would accompany him for as much as a month at a time. One day, when they had all gone for a walk in a Seattle park, Karen took too big a step running through the grass, tripped, and fell. She had a bump on her head and a nosebleed, and that evening Neil and Jan noticed that her eyes weren't focusing properly; a possible concussion, they thought. They took her immediately to a pediatrician, who advised them to take Karen to an eye doctor back home in California, which they did. In the next few days, Karen grew progressively worse . . . [and] X rays showed an inoperable brain tumor. The results [of attempts to reduce the size of the tumor with X-ray treatments] were encouraging; Karen learned to crawl again, then to walk, then to run and play, although she had a big bald spot on her head as a result of the X rays.

Sadly, however, the little girl's recovery was short-lived. Karen died on January 28, 1962, the Armstrongs' sixth wedding anniversary. She was not quite three years old.

Despite the lack of modern conveniences in their new home, its isolated yet tranquil setting among the Joshua trees suited the Armstrongs perfectly. Jan loved the clear desert air, and she could sit outside with her binoculars and watch the planes from Edwards hurtle overhead. Both the Armstrongs cherished their privacy, but each had tremendous warmth that they shared with their few close friends, sometimes in unexpected ways. After a successful first flight of an experimental aircraft, the NACA pilots often held a party to celebrate. According to Andrew Chaikin, these parties "usually saw Armstrong at the piano, pounding out a bit of ragtime; he might be the last to leave."[21] From the party, the couple would retreat to their home in the hills and their privacy once more. But world events in October 1957 changed the atmosphere not only at Edwards but in the Armstrong household as well.

SPUTNIK

On October 4, 1957, the Union of Soviet Socialist Republics (or the Soviet Union) launched the world's first artificial satellite, called Sputnik. About the size of a basketball and weighing 183 pounds, Sputnik orbited Earth every ninety-eight minutes. It was clearly visible in the night sky, and it transmitted a radio signal that allowed almost anyone to track its progress. Suddenly, the American public wanted to know how the Soviets had managed to launch an artificial satellite ahead of the United States.

Sputnik's success had caught the American scientific community off guard. The United States had planned to launch a much smaller satellite during 1958, but for many Americans, Sputnik demonstrated two things: the Soviet Union had the ability to launch a heavier payload into orbit, and the Soviets might follow this first satellite by placing nuclear weapons into orbit around the Earth.

The launch affected the community at Edwards in a small way at first. In 1958, Congress renamed the NACA and gave it a new mission. Now called the National Aeronautics and Space Administration (NASA), its mission was to move beyond experimental test flights to include flights in Earth orbit and perhaps into outer space.

Soon, the test pilots had a new aircraft with which they could undertake part of NASA's new mission by testing the bounds of Earth's atmosphere, and NASA had begun planning for a more advanced vehicle that might take them into space itself. The new vehicle was the X-15; after many years of planning, the concept was now an aircraft they could actually fly. The new concept under development was called Dynamic Soaring, or Dyna-Soar for short. And during the three years from 1959 to 1962, Neil Armstrong was intimately associated with both. The successes and failures of both, along with events at home, made these very pivotal years in Armstrong's life.

FLYING THE ROCKET PLANE

When NASA first started test flights of the X-15 in 1959, Armstrong learned its systems and behaviors through simulators and eventually through flying it himself. This revolutionary vehicle was basically a rocket engine with wings and was designed to travel up to Mach 7, or seven times the speed of sound, at an altitude of more than 250,000 feet. It was designed with controls that worked like a conventional airplane as well as steam-powered reaction controls that would help control the craft in the thin air of the upper atmosphere where normal airplane controls (such as ailerons, rudders, and flaps) would be ineffective.

The X-15 was launched from beneath the wing of a B-52 bomber at an altitude of 45,000 feet. Immediately after it was released from the bomber, the X-15 pilot ignited the rocket engine, and it hurtled into the sky. Once its fuel was exhausted, the pilot guided the craft back to earth in a controlled glide for a landing. The X-15 carried eighty-five seconds' worth of fuel; a typical flight lasted just eleven minutes from launch to touchdown. But the flights yielded amazing amounts of information about flight in the upper atmosphere as well as the effects of high speeds on pilots.

The extreme acceleration of the X-15 took the pilot through the sound barrier shortly after the flight began, eventually reaching more than Mach 5, or five times the speed of sound. During this high-speed sprint, the pilot experienced upward of five times the Earth's normal gravity (5Gs). For one test flight, Armstrong was assigned to test new specialized equipment, called the G limiter. It was designed to minimize the duration of the pilot's exposure to 5Gs, which would help keep the pilot from experiencing excess gravitational forces. In testing the new equipment, Armstrong set

the record for the longest X-15 flight. In addition, he reached the upper limits of the atmosphere.

To the Edge of Space

In April 1962, Armstrong began testing the new control equipment on the third X-15 plane. By this time, he had made hundreds of flights in the X-15, both flying the real aircraft and using the ground-based training simulators. On April 20, he boarded a B-52 to test the new X-15. When the rocket plane was launched from the B-52, he steadily climbed to an altitude of 207,000 feet, where the atmosphere is so thin that it is almost nonexistent.

At this altitude, nearly beyond the atmosphere, Armstrong kept trying to generate more G gravitational forces to get the G limiter to engage. He recalled that in so doing, "I got the nose up above the horizons," a maneuver he had done countless times in the simulators. However, in real flight, he discovered he was "skipping outside the atmosphere [where] . . . I had no aerodynamic controls. That was not a particular problem, because I still had reaction controls to use, but what I couldn't do is get back down in the atmosphere."[22]

He rolled the X-15 over, hoping that it would lose speed and then glide back into the atmosphere. But because he was at such a high altitude, the aircraft's wings were useless at helping him descend; in his words, "there was no air to bite into,"[23] so he just had to wait until his speed decreased and gravity began to pull the X-15 earthward.

Armstrong stands beside the experimental X-15 in 1960. The aircraft was designed to travel up to seven times the speed of sound.

Armstrong was out of radio contact with NASA until he started reentering the atmosphere. At this point, he regained communications, but what he heard from the ground told him that he was well outside his assigned flight path, having rocketed past the normal approach zone, gliding too high and too fast to begin usual approach spiral. Unable to turn as he flew past the south edge of Edwards, over Lancaster, Palmdale, and the San Gabriel Mountains, he was discovering that what worked in the simulator training was not working in reality.

His experience in the simulators led him to believe that he had enough airspeed to

G FORCES

Test pilots and astronauts work in an environment in which the pull of Earth's gravity can be increased, decreased, and eliminated altogether. In order to explain the various ways in which the human body reacts to these changes, scientists describe the varying degree of gravitational pull as G forces.

The normal force of gravity, which holds us to Earth's surface, is called 1G. A person weighing 150 pounds under the force of 1G feels like he or she weighs 150 pounds. In 2G conditions, that same person feels like he or she weighs three hundred pounds. Consequently, the person in a 2G environment finds it harder to use muscles in the legs, neck, or arms; the muscles are not accustomed to moving the increased weight of the body part. After prolonged exposure to increased G forces, the heart has difficulty continuing to pump blood to the body's extremities, like the legs and brain, and the pilot can lose consciousness.

Today, astronauts on the space shuttle experience a maximum of about 3Gs during launch. The X-15 contained specialized equipment that limited the pilot to less than 5Gs. Modern jet fighter pilots routinely work in conditions up to 5Gs and can undergo stresses up to 9Gs, depending on the tolerance of the aircraft. However, these pilots have specialized flight suits that decrease the effects of G forces on crucial muscles and that keep blood circulation going. Such suits had not been invented while the X-15 was in operation.

begin his turn, but during this flight the only way he could gain enough maneuverability to begin turning was to almost double his speed, by dropping the nose of the X-15. His flight had taken him roughly 45 miles south of Edwards, in the vicinity of Pasadena, California. But at least now he was able to turn back north toward Edwards. Almost thirty years after the flight, he recalled: "It wasn't clear at the time I made the turn whether I would be able to get back to Edwards. . . . [Eventually], I could see that we were going to make it back to Edwards, so I landed without incident on the south part of the lake."[24]

Armstrong succeeded in stretching the X-15's glide all the way back to the south end of the lake bed he had originally intended to land in. The pilots of the chase planes escorted him back to Edwards and later said that he had cleared the tops of the Joshua trees at the edge of the lake by only about 100 feet. The flight ended after 12.5 minutes and was the longest X-15 flight of the entire research program. It also demonstrated Armstrong's ability both to keep his cool during a stressful flight and to call on his extensive training to remedy a situation.

By the time of this flight, Armstrong was the leading candidate to become the chief pilot of the X-15 program. Yet he was also involved in the Dyna-Soar project, which was particularly interesting because it might lead to flights that would orbit Earth.

DYNA-SOAR AND BEYOND

The designers of the Dynamic Soaring, or Dyna-Soar, craft envisioned it as a winged vehicle that could be launched into the upper atmosphere by a rocket booster and then return to Earth as an airplane, much as the modern space shuttle is used. Later, as rocket technology advanced and the United States began launching satellites into orbit, the design evolved into an orbiting vehicle. Armstrong spent several years at Edwards working on this program, studying different design concepts and determining how to modify an existing aircraft design into the Dyna-Soar.

However, by 1962, he was concerned that the work at NASA's High Speed Flight Station at Edwards was no longer leading the field of flight research. He thought the Dyna-Soar concept was promising, yet he wondered if the craft would ever become a reality. Meanwhile, NASA seemed to be reaching new heights in research and accomplishments with its manned orbital program, based in Houston, Texas.

The Houston program, called Mercury, was putting men in orbit and returning them safely to Earth. The USSR had achieved the first manned orbit, when Yury Gagarin orbited Earth on April 12, 1961; NASA's first manned orbit came the following February, when John Glenn circled Earth three times before returning.

Astronaut John Glenn, the first American to orbit Earth, climbs into his capsule. Glenn's achievement inspired Armstrong to apply for NASA's space program.

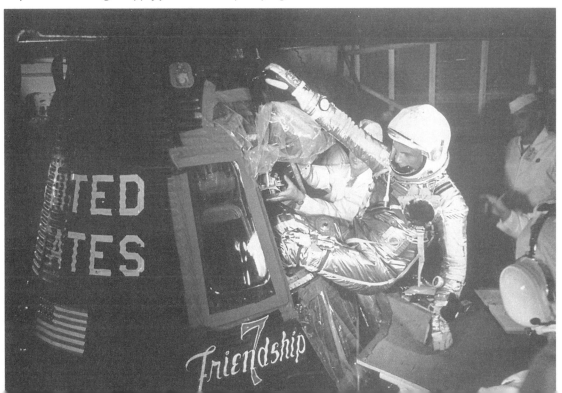

The achievements of these astronauts intrigued Armstrong. He had had no real interest in the Mercury program when it was first announced in 1959, mostly because he felt, as many other pilots did, that computers would control the spacecraft. The astronauts, according to a phrase that the pilots at Edwards often used, would be no more than "Spam in a can."[25] However, Glenn's flight demonstrated that this was hardly the case, as he had taken control of his craft to manually operate the small maneuvering rockets that adjusted the capsule's orientation in space.

Now, given the success of the Mercury flights, Armstrong began to reassess his opinion of the space program, as well as his career options. And the same week in April 1962 that he flew the X-15 to the edge of space, NASA issued an announcement calling for volunteers for the next group of astronauts to participate in Mercury's suc-

"MAX PECK"

When Deke Slayton offered an astronaut position to U.S. Navy pilot Jim Lovell on September 14, 1962, he told Lovell to check into the Rice Hotel in Houston under the name Max Peck. In the book *Lost Moon*, Lovell and coauthor Jeffrey Kluger describe Lovell's arrival:

> "At the hotel, [Lovell] paid the [taxi] driver, walked inside, and looked around. There was still no sign of Deke or anyone else who looked remotely attached to NASA. Feeling more than a little lost, Lovell went to the desk with as much nonchalance as he could muster and nodded hello to the clerk.
>
> 'I have a reservation for a single room,' Lovell said. 'I'm Max Peck.'
>
> The clerk was a girl of barely college age. 'Excuse me? You're who?'
>
> 'I'm Mr. Max—I mean, Mr. Peck. I'm Max Peck.'
>
> 'Uh, I don't think so,' said the girl. . . .
>
> All at once, from behind the desk, another hotel employee appeared. . . . 'I'll take care of this, Sheila,' he said to the girl, and then turned to Lovell. 'Glad you could make it, Mr. Peck. Here's your key, and do let us know if anything is not to your satisfaction.'"

Later, Lovell went to the lobby, and discovered that all the men that NASA had brought to the hotel had been told to be "Max Peck." He thought the cloak-and-dagger routine was silly, but eventually he found himself surrounded by the other eight: Navy men Pete Conrad and John Young; Ed White, Frank Borman, Jim McDivitt, and Tom Stafford from the Air Force; Elliot See, a civilian test pilot for General Electric; and, arriving last, Neil Armstrong.

cessors, the Gemini and Apollo programs. Armstrong decided to apply.

AN IMPORTANT DECISION

Several factors led Armstrong to apply for the Houston program. The X-15 program, although successful, was Earth-bound; it would never achieve orbit. Dyna-Soar was dragging on, with no real end in sight. But the stated objective of the Houston programs was to put a man on the Moon and return him safely to Earth, and he told Bill Dana, a fellow NASA pilot, as much: "space is the frontier, and that is where I intend to go."[26]

Armstrong and 252 other candidates applied; NASA's chief astronaut, Donald K. "Deke" Slayton, supervised the selec-

tion process. By mid-September 1962, he and his committee had decided on nine candidates. Neil Armstrong was one of them.

Thus, the Armstrongs would soon be leaving Edwards, his job site for seven years. He and Jan had made several close friends there, and they had lived in and worked on their remote desert home in the mountains since 1957. Their son, Eric (nicknamed "Ricky"), and their daughter, Karen, had been born during the family's time in California. Now they were faced with packing up their belongings and moving to Texas. While Jan stayed behind to supervise the moving process, Neil Armstrong went ahead to Houston to start his new job, as one of the "New Nine" U.S. astronauts.

4 Dreams of Flying in Space

In the fall of 1962, as Neil and Jan Armstrong moved their family to Houston, the United States and the Soviet Union were locked in a competition called the 'space race,' to see which nation had the superior space technology. Both nations were developing new spacecraft and hardware to make putting men into orbit easier and safer. Both were refining training techniques, and both were gathering scientific information about the effects of weightlessness in orbit on the human body.

In 1961, American president John F. Kennedy announced that the United States should "commit itself to achieving the goal, before the decade is out, of landing a man on the moon and returning him safely to earth."[27] Kennedy's challenge was one of the reasons that the National Aeronautics and Space Administration (NASA) recruited additional astronauts, and it was why Neil Armstrong, one of the "New Nine," reported to Houston for astronaut training.

TRAINING FOR SPACE

As the New Nine joined the "Original Seven," the Mercury astronauts, at the end of 1962, the Mercury program was still in full swing, but in mid-1963 the new two-man Gemini program was slated to begin. No one knew who would fly on the Gemini missions, but the new astronauts figured they had been hired for those flights. Until the assignments came, Armstrong and the other astronauts underwent rigorous training regimens to prepare for space flight.

When the space program began, NASA was unsure how much stress a flight would put on an astronaut's body. The lift off and reentry phases were thought to be the most demanding, and so NASA subjected the Mercury astronauts to intense G-force training. However, by the time the New Nine arrived, NASA had learned a great deal about how a human body reacts in the weightlessness of space, and astronaut training concentrated on technological training. The astronauts attended specialized lectures and meetings about manned space flight. They were taken on survival training field trips to different environments around the world (such as jungles and deserts), where they learned how to live off the land in case they landed in unexpected territory. In addition, each astronaut was in charge of a specialized discipline within the preparations for the Gemini program.

Armstrong was in charge of developing and designing the trainers and simulators the astronauts would use during the preparations for the flights to the Moon. In a 1963 article for *Life* magazine, he described his duties:

> In my particular area of specialization . . . which is to perfect the trainers and simulators we need to practice for moon flight, we are trying to simulate tasks that man has never done before. I do not have an assigned checklist of things to do. I simply have to take a hard look at the missions we have planned and decide for myself which areas we need to work on and how we'll do it. . . . It so happens that pilots are notoriously leery of [simulators]. If you want to learn to fly a DC-3, for example, the best thing would be to go out in a DC-3 and practice. But we can't

The New Nine NASA astronauts pose with models of the Mercury, Apollo, and Gemini spacecrafts. Armstrong is in the front row, second from the right.

go out and practice landing on the moon. We have to re-create the conditions as realistically as possible in a kind of serious let's pretend.[28]

THE GOALS OF GEMINI

Success in Armstrong's assigned disciplines simulation and training were crucial to the accomplishment of Gemini's goals. For example, NASA hoped the missions would prove that a human being could spend several days in space without suffering physical or mental fatigue; this would demonstrate that the astronauts could undertake a voyage to the Moon and back over a period of more than a week. NASA also planned to practice a technique called rendezvous, in which two spacecraft approached and docked (became attached) while in orbit; this skill would be crucial in the years ahead during the Apollo missions. Finally, the planners hoped to perform several extravehicular activities (or EVA) in which an astronaut in a spacesuit and tethered to the capsule left the spacecraft and worked in space.

Michael Collins (center) and Buzz Aldrin (right) joined the Gemini program in 1963. They and Armstrong (left) would eventually comprise the crew of Apollo 11.

By the time the first unmanned Gemini test flights lifted off in the spring of 1964, only three of the original Mercury Seven astronauts were still in the program, and the New Nine were no longer new. NASA had hired fourteen more astronauts in the fall of 1963, including two U.S. Air Force officers, Edwin E. "Buzz" Aldrin Jr. and Michael Collins, both of whom would eventually play a large part in Neil Armstrong's life.

The new astronauts worked to master their occupations as Armstrong and the others continued to concentrate on the upcoming Gemini program. However, one night in 1964 reminded the Armstrongs that sometimes everyday events occur and the unexpected happens.

FAMILY MATTERS

By the spring of 1964, life in the Armstrong household had settled into a routine. The couple was comfortably settled into the NASA family of the Manned Space Center. They had a new son, Mark, who had been born in 1963. They had built a home in the suburban Houston community of El Lago, where many of the other astronauts lived, including next-door neighbors Ed and Pat White, with whom the Armstrongs had bought the land.

The Armstrongs' new house in El Lago, which reflected the appreciation for Japanese culture that Neil had developed in visits to Japan during the Korean War, caught fire one early morning in 1964.

The fire department arrived too late to save the home and its collection of family mementos, photos, papers, and Neil's trea-

While Armstrong trained to be an astronaut, his wife Jan ran the household and cared for their sons, Eric and Mark.

sured copies of old aviation magazines, but the Armstrongs escaped unharmed. They built a new house on the same lot, planted a Japanese garden with ivy around it, and returned to a Japanese motif in some of the new home's designs.

FIRE AT THE ARMSTRONG HOUSE

In Gene Farmer and Dora Jane Hamblin's book First on the Moon, *Jan Armstrong recalled the eventful night when their first home in El Lago caught fire.*

[Neil] went out the door . . . and he came back and said the house was on fire. . . . So I . . . fumbled for the light—and Neil told me to call the fire department. I couldn't get the operator on the telephone at 3 A.M. . . . Neil had gone in for [their son] Marky. I ran to the back of the house, and I was banging on the fence calling for Pat and Ed White, who lived next door. . . . Ed came bolting over the fence. I don't know how he did it, but he took one leap, and he was over. He got the hoses out immediately. . . . [Neil] was standing there calling for somebody to come and get Mark because he was—what, ten months old?—and he couldn't put him down because he was afraid Mark would crawl into the swimming pool and drown. By this time I could hear the fire engines on the way—Pat White had turned in the alarm. This whole wall was red, and the glass was cracking on the windows. I can remember Ed White calling me. He was saying: here, you hold the hose; I'll get Mark. Neil had gone in for Ricky, who was just awakening at the time. And I was standing with the hose, the concrete was burning my feet, and we had to keep watering the concrete so we could stand there.

It was a busy time for the Armstrongs. As 1965 began, Neil was continuing his astronaut training and his simulator development for Gemini and Apollo. Jan was running the household and caring for their two small boys, and both were working hard to make their new house a home. And for NASA, the first manned Gemini flights began. However, during the gap between the end of Mercury and the beginning of Gemini, the Soviet Union's space program had continued to post remarkable achievements, reminding NASA that the nation was still a challenger for the control of Earth orbit—and perhaps outer space as well.

THE SOVIET CHALLENGE

From May 1963 until March 1965, the Soviets continued to achieve firsts in Earth orbit. As early as August 1962, the Soviet space program had launched two capsules into orbit, *Vostok 3* and *Vostok 4*. In June 1963, Valentina Tereskova became the first woman to orbit the globe. October 12, 1964, marked the first orbit of three Soviet men in space. In March 1965, from *Voskhod 2*, cosmonaut Alexei Leonov performed the first-ever EVA. Many observers of the programs of the two competing nations thought that the Soviets' knowledge of science and technology was far superior to the Americans'.

The Soviet Union's accomplishments burst on the world scene sporadically. Each flight took place with little or no advance warning. Each success was celebrated with great fanfare by the Soviet press and gained increasing attention from newspapers, radio, and television from the rest of the world. However, failures of testing procedures and equipment were buried in secrecy. The day-to-day work of the Soviet scientists and cosmonauts behind the scenes was relatively free from outside scrutiny. But the U.S. program was, for the most part, conducted in the open. And soon NASA had its own string of accomplishments.

BACKUP AND CREW

After two successful test flights of unmanned Gemini systems in 1964, the first two-person crew flew into orbit on March 23, 1965. *Gemini 3* astronauts Gus Grissom (one of the Mercury Seven) and John Young (one of the New Nine) orbited the earth just three times. However, less than three months later, *Gemini IV*, with the Armstrongs' neighbor Ed White and Jim McDivitt aboard, made eighty-two orbits and stayed in space for over four days. (NASA changed its designations for the Gemini missions from Arabic to Roman numerals after *Gemini 3*.) Additionally, White accomplished NASA's first

EVA. The successes of the first two manned Gemini flights demonstrated that the United States was still committed to space flight.

They also marked the beginning of a rotation of astronauts. Deke Slayton had realized when the new astronauts were hired that NASA needed a comprehensive schedule for their training, and he assigned Armstrong the task of determining how many crews and astronauts NASA would need for the entire Gemini program. "We actually had so few people," Armstrong recalls, "that almost everybody was assigned all the time. In that period I would come off one crew assignment, and within a few weeks I'd be assigned to something else, and that endured throughout the entire Gemini program."[29]

Slayton used this information to build a rotation system for flight assignments. Each Gemini flight had two astronauts that trained for the particular mission as the prime crew, as well as two additional astronauts who were the crew's backup. The backup crew trained for the same mission as the prime crew, used the same equipment, and was required to know the flight's goals and objectives as thoroughly.

Even before *Gemini 3* flew, Slayton assigned astronauts to future missions as crews and backups. Eventually, the schedule was designed so that a backup crew trained for a mission, skipped two missions, and then became the prime crew for the next mission. Both prime and backup crews consisted of a commander and a pilot; the commander was in charge of the flight. Armstrong's first assignment to a backup crew came for *Gemini V*. His dreams of flying in space were coming closer to reality.

Gemini V

For the mission of *Gemini V*, Armstrong was paired with Elliott See as backup to Gordon Cooper and Pete Conrad; Armstrong served as the commander on the backup crew. Armstrong was thrilled to get the assignment:

> Well, I was really pleased to be assigned to a flight. . . . It was quite a change from the time before, when we were working lots of general projects and trying to build pieces here and there, to all of a sudden having a pretty much complete focus on achieving the objectives of that flight, which was originally intended to be a one-week-long flight, [the first] long-duration flight.[30]

The four *Gemini V* astronauts spent months on end flying back and forth from Houston to the McDonnell Douglas Aircraft factory in St. Louis, Missouri, where the *Gemini V* capsule was being manufactured. They worked with the technicians who built the spacecraft, and participated in its testing, much of which took place at 2 A.M. or in the predawn hours.

The demands of preparing for a space mission were tremendous. The astronauts tried to get home to see their families on weekends, but sometimes even that was impossible. Jan Armstrong remembered that Neil would come home exhausted and would read a stack of papers from NASA while he ate dinner. Early the next morning, he would head back to the Manned Space Center with only coffee for breakfast. The work of the backup crew continued even as the flight was in progress; after attending

Gemini V's launch on August 21, 1965, Armstrong and See helped NASA and the astronauts tackle some problems that Cooper and Conrad were encountering in space. Additionally, Armstrong served as one of three capsule communicators during the flight, relaying instructions from the ground to the spacecraft.

When *Gemini V* landed, Cooper and Conrad had completed a mission that had lasted almost eight days and had made 120 orbits. In the record-breaking flight, the two astronauts had surpassed the Soviet Union's duration record by more than two days.

A New Assignment

The end of the flight also meant it was time for new assignments. Slayton assigned Armstrong and Dave Scott to the *Gemini VIII* mission, which had as its objective a major task that NASA saw as essential for a mission to the Moon. Armstrong and Scott were to be the first to rendezvous and dock with an unmanned *Agena* rocket. The flight was scheduled for March 1966.

Armstrong and Scott plunged into their mission training. They trained for weightlessness by spending hours in KC-135 aircraft flying parabolas over Texas; the planes repeatedly flew in a steep climb and then nosed over. In the few seconds before the planes began their descent, the pull of gravity was almost zero and the astronauts had a short period of weightlessness. They worked endlessly in the simulators for the flight. They studied the mission goals and

GEMINI PROGRAM–MANNED MISSIONS
MARCH 1965 TO NOVEMBER 1966

NASA
GEMINI

Flight	Crew	Launch Date
Gemini 3	Gus Grissom, John Young	March 1965
Gemini IV	Jim McDivitt, Ed White	June 1965
Gemini V	Gordon Cooper, Pete Conrad	August 1965
Gemini VI-A	Wally Schirra, Tom Stafford	December 1965
Gemini VII	Frank Borman, Jim Lovell	December 1965
Gemini VIII	Neil Armstrong, Dave Scott	March 1966
Gemini IX-A	Tom Stafford, Gene Cernan	June 1966
Gemini X	John Young, Michael Collins	July 1966
Gemini XI	Pete Conrad, Richard Cooper	September 1966
Gemini XII	Jim Lovell, Buzz Aldrin	November 1966

objectives intently and worked through many emergency situations, trying to prepare for any possible contingency.

AN EMERGENCY IN SPACE

When Armstrong and Scott lifted off from Cape Kennedy, Florida, on March 16, 1966, the Gemini program was putting people in orbit about once every two months. The ambitious schedule was necessary if the United States was going to fulfill President Kennedy's 1961 challenge to land a man on the Moon before the end of the decade.

Many of the goals of the Gemini missions were a direct result of that challenge and were seen as a prelude to the Apollo missions. *Gemini VIII*'s rendezvous and docking with the *Agena* were a prelude to the Apollo program's rendezvous and docking of vehicles that would orbit and land on the Moon.

The *Agena* and *Gemini VIII* were launched about ninety minutes apart on March 16. Armstrong and Scott had no trouble finding the rocket once they were in orbit and maneuvering their capsule into docking position. They accomplished the docking itself easily, but soon something went wrong:

DAVE SCOTT'S ACCOUNTING

In 1966, Dave Scott kept a careful record of the many hours he spent in astronaut training, which included the time he and Neil Armstrong trained for Gemini VIII. *In Farmer and Hamblin's book* First on the Moon:

[S]ystem briefing and lectures, 300 hours; spacecraft testing, 370 hours; simulations on lunar modules, lunar landing research vehicles, mockups and command and service modules, 680 hours; operational briefings, 270 hours; mission equipment development, 350 hours; flying check rides and personal travel in T-33 and T-38 jets, 200 hours; flying helicopters, 40 hours.

Armstrong and Dave Scott study the interior of the Gemini command module. Scott kept a detailed record of their astronaut training.

Scott noticed that the docked spacecraft were beginning to tumble, as if the capsule were somersaulting end over end.

TUMBLING OUT OF CONTROL AND IN THE DARK

When they first noticed the tumbling, they were on the night side of the Earth, which meant that Armstrong and Scott could not see any of the landmarks that would have helped them evaluate their situation. They thought that a maneuvering jet called a thruster on the *Agena* might be the culprit, so Scott tried to stabilize the tumbling, using the thrusters on the *Agena*, but without success. As the tumbling became more and more violent, they made the decision to separate from the *Agena*. But once they undocked, the tumbling only got worse. At that point, they realized that the problem was with their capsule.

The tumbling was extremely disorienting. The capsule was not only rolling like a barrel but also somersaulting end over end. Armstrong remarked to Scott half-jokingly, "I gotta cage my eyeballs."[31] He tried methodically to figure out which thruster was causing the problems but was having no success. Moreover, the rate of tumbling was increasing, and they were out of communication with Houston.

In those early days of space flight, some areas of the astronauts' orbits were out of range of the network of receiving stations around the world. As the tumbling became alarming, Armstrong and Scott were passing over mainland China where NASA had no monitoring stations; the ground stations in Australia were out of range of *Gemini VIII*'s signals. Eventually, the astronauts came in range of a radio ship stationed in the Pacific Ocean, which relayed their news to Mission Control in Houston.

THE DECISION TO ABORT

When Armstrong's words, "We've got serious problems, we're tumbling end over end,"[32] were relayed from the radio ship to Mission Control, *Gemini VIII* had been out of control for several minutes. The G forces were becoming difficult to handle. Both astronauts were worried about losing consciousness. They were now tumbling at the rate of about one somersault a second. Armstrong made the decision to try to stabilize the capsule by firing its retrorockets, which under normal circumstances were used only for reentry purposes. It was a drastic measure, but it worked. Soon, Armstrong had the craft under control.

As the capsule crossed over North America, both Mission Control and the astronauts realized that they would have to end on the next orbit. Scott was particularly disappointed that he would not be able to perform his scheduled EVA, but both he and Armstrong understood that Mission Control saw their safety as paramount. NASA could schedule *Gemini VIII*'s goals for a later flight.

Armstrong and Scott splashed down in the Pacific Ocean. A U.S. Navy ship picked up the two astronauts, who were weary from their ordeal and slightly seasick from the high seas, but they were physically unharmed by their harrowing experience.

REENTRY AND RECOVERY

With Gemini VIII's *mission cut short by the malfunctioning thruster, Armstrong and Scott still had the challenging reentry and splashdown to accomplish before they could reach safety. In* On the Shoulders of Titans, *Barton C. Hacker and James M. Grimwood recount* Gemini VIII's *return to Earth:*

Everything clicked off properly during descent. As they neared a landing, Armstrong asked his partner, "Do you [see] water out there?" Looking into the first faint light of dawn, Scott replied, "All I see is haze." Then his voice quickened, "Oh, yes, there's water! It's water!" Less than two minutes later, Scott yelled, "LANDING—SAFE." The flight had lasted 10 hours 41 minutes 26 seconds.

The crew went quickly through the postlanding checklist, putting switches and valves in their correct positions. . . . Houston Flight Control had told them the rescue planes would get to them shortly and the [U.S. Navy rescue ship USS] *Mason* should reach them in three hours. . . .

Several aircraft, including two HC-54 Rescuemasters—one from Naha Air Base, Okinawa, and the other from Tachikawa Air Base, Japan—had raced to fetch the crew. The HC-54 from Naha got there first. Suddenly the pilot shouted, "I got it!" He had seen the spacecraft, with its main parachute in full bloom, drifting to the ocean's surface. Three pararescuemen were equipped and ready to jump. Armstrong and Scott saw one of the three as he parachuted down. Because of the waves, the [Navy rescue swimmers] had trouble hooking the flotation collar to the spacecraft. The rough sea also made them queasy, a feeling shared by the astronauts. But the swimmers persisted and secured the collar within 45 minutes of spacecraft landing. . . . Three hours later, as promised, the *Mason* pulled alongside and fastened a line to the spacecraft. . . . On deck, the tired astronauts managed smiles and greetings for the welcoming sailors.

Navy rescue swimmers stand on the flotation collar they attached to Gemini VIII, *as Armstrong and Scott wait for the rescue ship.*

Additionally, their calm assessment of the situation during postmission studies aided NASA significantly.

The Lessons of *Gemini VIII*

Gemini VIII taught NASA some important lessons. The agency's technicians soon confirmed what Armstrong and Scott had suspected; their number eight thruster had been firing constantly, as if it had been stuck in the on position. Some rewiring allowed later Gemini astronauts to turn off their thrusters completely if necessary. The emergency reentry, after only seven orbits and only ten hours, tested and proved the effectiveness of the agency's partnership with the Navy for crew recovery throughout the Pacific.

Perhaps the most important lesson from *Gemini VIII* came from how the men approached their troubling situation. The steps that Armstrong and Scott took to regain control of their capsule vindicated the decision to put the astronauts in control of their spacecraft. Armstrong's quick responses and cool reactions to the crisis proved that these men were truly not "Spam in a can." Indeed, had they not survived the ordeal, the American-manned space program might have ground to a halt. Neil Armstrong's piloting skills had saved the day, and the successful responses by the astronauts and NASA to the *Gemini VIII* crisis paved the way for Apollo.

Chapter

5 Dreams of the Moon

Gemini VIII marked the last time Neil Armstrong went into space on a Gemini mission. The program had four more missions planned before it ended in 1966, but NASA passed much of its attention to the planned Apollo missions. The hardware and equipment of Apollo were taking shape. The new Saturn booster rockets were being assembled and tested; the command modules, built to hold three astronauts, were being constructed by North American Aviation in California; and the lunar modules, designed to take two astronauts to the surface of the Moon, were being manufactured by Grumman Aircraft in New York State. Around the country, thousands of men and women were striving to fulfill President Kennedy's goals. Activity at the Manned Space Center at Houston was at its height.

The first test of an unmanned Apollo flight, using a Saturn IB booster system, came on February 26, 1966; the suborbital flight was a success. NASA looked forward to two more unmanned test flights before launching the first manned orbital flight, designated *Apollo 1*. Deke Slayton called 1966 "NASA's best year,"[33] and it seemed as if the U.S. dream of reaching the Moon by the end of the 1960s might come true.

However, a tragedy almost brought an end to the entire space program.

THE FIRE OF *APOLLO 1*

On January 27, 1967 astronauts Gus Grissom, Ed White, and Roger Chaffee were training for the flight of *Apollo 1*. Their flight was to be a fourteen-day orbital mission to test the command module equipment, but before they could lift off, they had a large number of tests to perform while on the ground. One, called a "plugs out" test, took place on January 27. With the capsule fully pressurized and the astronauts wearing their pressure suits, the controllers simulated a launch countdown with the rocket and its capsule disconnected from external power sources, as they would be during a launch.

The test did not go well from the start. The afternoon dragged into early evening. Communications problems plagued the crew and the technicians in the building nearby. Grissom questioned how they were going to get to the Moon "if we can't talk between two buildings." Shortly after that, Chaffee announced, "Fire in the spacecraft."[34] In the next eighteen seconds, a horrific fire consumed the oxygen inside the capsule and all three astronauts died—not from the flames but from suffocation.

Because of the intense heat of the fire, it took several hours for the technicians on the launch pad to get close enough to the capsule to remove the men. They discovered that the crew had tried to remove their hatch, but without success.

The fire had occurred around 6:30 P.M. eastern time. Word spread quickly but quietly through the NASA community. Neil Armstrong, who along with several other astronauts, had been present at the White House when President Lyndon Johnson had signed the Outer Space Treaty, heard the shocking news in a Washington hotel.

The astronauts were fully aware of the risks of their occupation. Many, like Armstrong, had been test pilots and had seen or heard of fellow pilots dying during tests. Still, it hurt to lose their friends.

LOST FRIENDS

For the Armstrongs, the *Apollo 1* fire hit home in many ways. Neil Armstrong and Ed White had been friends since the Houston

Astronauts Ed White, Gus Grissom, and Roger Chaffee (left to right) were killed during a preflight test of Apollo 1. The tragedy nearly ended NASA's space program.

days; the Whites had helped Neil and Jan during their house fire in 1964. Armstrong had also known Gus Grissom for many years. Later, he recalled that it was a very traumatic time:

> I suppose that you're more likely to accept the loss of a friend in flight, but it really hurt to lose them in a ground test. . . . I mean, [it happened] because we didn't do the right thing somehow. That's doubly, doubly traumatic. . . . That's not the way it's supposed to happen. . . . It just hurts.[35]

Armstrong and the other astronauts flew back to Houston the day after the accident and began to wonder what the future held for the Apollo program and for NASA in general. Some members of Congress started questioning whether NASA should be shut down, but within a month, the space agency had begun an investigation of its own procedures.

Time to Regroup, Reevaluate, Resume

During the investigation, several teams at NASA and at North American Aviation, the firm that had built the capsule that burned, analyzed their previous decisions and policies. The teams discovered that changes needed to be made concerning crew safety and the new developing technologies. For example, the design of the capsule's door (or hatch) needed to be revised to allow easier opening, and the quality of wiring needed to be upgraded.

This period of reevaluation led to a new spirit of confidence at NASA. People seemed to have a new sense of mission. They still wanted to reach the Moon in time to meet Kennedy's challenge; they still wanted to get there before the Soviets; but now, they also wanted to get there to honor the memories of Grissom, White, and Chaffee. Additionally, the private contractors also felt a renewed commitment to their jobs and worked even harder to meet NASA's new construction and safety specifications.

Meanwhile, the engineers developing the new *Saturn V* rocket systems continued to refine the systems' designs. The *Saturn V* first flew in November 1967, and the dream of reaching the Moon seemed just a bit closer to reality.

Training for the Moon with the "Flying Bedstead"

Until the new rockets were ready, Armstrong and the other astronauts had a variety of training tools available. One new device had been invented by a partnership of NASA engineers at Edwards Air Force Base and the aviation division of General Electric Company. It was called the lunar landing research vehicle (LLRV). The LLRV was basically a General Electric jet engine mounted vertically on a frame with legs, with many control and maneuvering thruster jets positioned around, below, and on top of the frame. The pilot's seat in the front of the craft was armed with an ejection system. The craft was designed to simulate the last few minutes of a lunar landing, in which the lunar module was hovering and de-

JAN ARMSTRONG AND PAT WHITE, JANUARY 27, 1967

The wives of the astronauts were a close-knit group. Brought together by their husbands' careers, they had many things in common. The Astronaut Office understood the value of having a friend on hand when bad news came and made sure one of the other wives was visiting the victim's wife when its representative delivered the news. When the Apollo 1 *fire occurred, NASA officials moved quickly to ensure that the wives of Gus Grissom, Ed White, and Roger Chaffee were not alone. In* A Man on the Moon, *author Andrew Chaikin describes that evening:*

[Astronauts Alan Bean and Michael Collins] agreed that Bean would coordinate astronauts and wives to go to the homes of the dead pilots. Bean called his wife, Sue, and sent her to the home of Martha Chaffee until Collins could get there. Wally Schirra's wife, Jo, and Chuck Berry, the space center's chief physician, would go to Betty Grissom's. Neil Armstrong's wife, Jan, would go to her next-door neighbor Pat White's, and [astronaut] Bill Anders . . . would follow. . . . What was difficult—the hardest thing Anders would ever do—was to go to the house of this attractive woman in her thirties who was raising two children, bearing bad news. A short while ago Pat had picked up her daughter from a ballet lesson. When she arrived home . . . Jan . . . was waiting silently for her. She must have been surprised, then confused—Ed was at the Cape, he wasn't flying tonight—and then she must have filled with dread. But it wasn't up to one astronaut's wife to tell another that her darkest nightmare had come true. That task most often fell to other astronauts. Anders rang the doorbell.

scending gently. Because it had four legs that stretched out and down from the frame, in the words of one astronaut, "like an old brass bed frame,"[36] it was called it the "flying bedstead."

NASA modified several of the LLRVs, renamed them the lunar landing training vehicles (LLTVs), and brought them to Ellington Air Force Base near Houston. Slayton picked two astronauts he felt were most likely destined for early lunar landing missions, Pete Conrad and Neil Armstrong, and assigned them to learn how to fly them.

The LLTV was a tricky machine. The main jet engine generated the necessary thrust to move vertically, but the machine's main engine also helped simulate the reduced gravity of the Moon by keeping a constant thrust downward. In training, the astronaut flew the LLTV to an altitude of about five hundred feet and then switched to lunar simulation mode. The main engine neutralized five-sixths of the vehicle's weight to simulate the lunar gravity (which is one-sixth that of Earth), and the astronaut then tried to land, controlling descent by throttling

AFTER *APOLLO 1*

Through the spring of 1967, NASA investigated the Apollo 1 *accident. In* Footprints on the Moon, *Associated Press writer John Barbour summed up what had caused the fire, who was at fault, and what needed to be done to make the Apollo capsule safe to fly:*

Technicians inspect the burned Apollo 1 *command module.*

In the next self-critical months, more than 1,500 experts pored over the sooted remains of the *Apollo 1* spaceship. The fire was re-enacted in another spacecraft. After 10 weeks, the board produced its report, a masterpiece of introspection. It found both the space agency and North American [Aviation] guilty of poor management, carelessness, negligence, design deficiencies, and a failure to consider the safety of the astronauts adequately. The board decided the likely cause of the fire was faulty wiring, and an exposed arc of electricity that ignited materials in the spacecraft. . . . The board ordered major changes in design: sheathing with metal all wiring previously exposed, replacement of virtually all flammable materials in the cabin with flame-resistant materials, better communications, better armor on joints to prevent leakage, new nonflammable spacesuits and, importantly, a gas-operated hatch that could be opened in less than seven seconds compared to the *Apollo 1* double hatch that took 90 seconds to open under normal circumstances.

There were dozens of other changes in fire-proofing and failure-proofing, and a lot more work to be done before Apollo would fly.

two downward-facing rocket engines and using the control thrusters to control the LLTV's orientation. The LLTV seemed to be constantly in motion—not just up and down, but side to side and left and right—during landing simulations.

Author D.C. Agle writes that although the LLTV "quickly earned a reputation as a valuable training tool, it was also regarded as squirrely and unforgiving."[37]

On his twenty-first flight in the LLTV, Armstrong discovered how "squirrelly and unforgiving" the bedstead could be.

PUNCHING OUT

On May 6, 1968, Armstrong traveled to Ellington for another flight in the LLTV. By now, the *Saturn V* assemblies had undergone two unmanned flights (known as *Apollo 5* and *Apollo 6*), and NASA was planning to launch a manned flight in November. The manned portion of Apollo seemed back on track, and the astronauts stepped up their training for the Moon missions, in the simulators and in the LLTVs.

Armstrong was set to simulate the final portion of a lunar descent that day. He descended from about 500 feet to about 200 feet, and all appeared normal. The vehicle suddenly and unexpectedly pitched forward, and he was unable to control the craft with the maneuvering jets. At about 100 feet, he activated the ejection seat and, in pilot's slang, he "punched out." Then, moments before the LLTV crashed and exploded in flames, Armstrong parachuted to safety.

The lunar landing training vehicle (LLTV) consisted of a jet engine mounted on a frame with legs. The LLTV was designed to allow astronauts to practice landing on the Moon.

Initially, NASA wondered if the crash was due to a design flaw in the lunar module design, as the lunar module was planned to descend to the Moon in the same way the LLTV descended to Earth. But after an investigation, the accident was traced to a helium tank aboard the LLTV that had worked improperly, and the LLTV training continued.

THE LUNAR MODULE SIMULATOR

Although the LLTV was an invaluable training device, it could not simulate all the controls, switches, and computer operations that would exist in the final lunar module (LM). There were simply far too many. So for that, a full-scale reproduction of the LM was constructed, in which the astronauts could simulate their descents and landings.

This simulator did not move. Instead, a camera mounted above a lunar landscape moved in response to the commands the astronauts gave to the LM's controls. In this simulator, the astronauts practiced bringing the LM to a successful lunar landing.

Occasionally, however, simulator technicians who had programmed the simulation threw in an unexpected "emergency," such as a faulty thruster or a failure of the landing radar system, to see how the astronauts would cope. NASA hoped to train for every situation that might occur and hoped that if something did go wrong with the hardware, the astronauts could deal with it. Endless numbers of simulations ended with crash landings, but it was all worthwhile. There would be no way to

"punch out" from the real LM above the Moon.

By the summer of 1968, Armstrong had spent countless hours in the LM simulator, training in the commander's position. When Slayton announced crew assignments for the first four-manned Apollo missions in July 1968, Armstrong was named as backup commander for *Apollo 9*, with Buzz Aldrin as his LM pilot and Fred Haise as his command module pilot. His dream of going to the Moon seemed just a bit closer to coming true. However, less than a month later, the crew assignments changed, because of problems with a craft called *Spider*.

PROBLEMS WITH *SPIDER*

Spider was the name that astronauts Jim McDivitt, Dave Scott, and Rusty Schweickart had given to the first fully functional LM constructed by Grumman Aircraft. Their flight assignment was to test it in orbit, but problems kept arising while it was still in development. Systems failed, electronic malfunctions occurred, and parts broke during stress tests. Time was running short, and by the summer of 1968, less than eighteen months remained to meet President Kennedy's goal. It eventually became apparent that *Spider* would not be ready to fly when the launch date came.

NASA officials came up with an intriguing alternative to postponing the mission until *Spider* was ready, which could be as late as early 1969. Rather than halt the flight schedule while they waited for the LM to be ready, officials came up with an

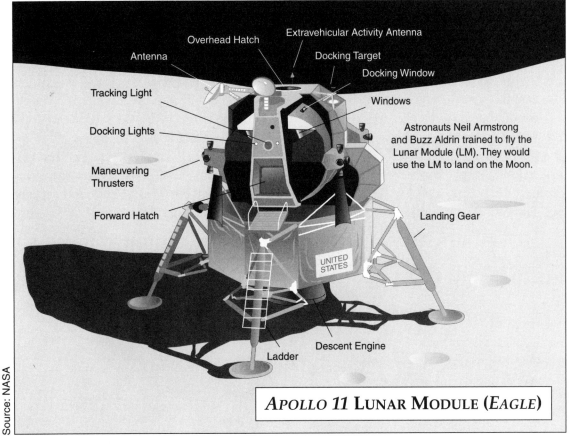

Overhead Hatch
Extravehicular Activity Antenna
Antenna
Docking Target
Docking Window
Tracking Light
Windows
Docking Lights
Astronauts Neil Armstrong and Buzz Aldrin trained to fly the Lunar Module (LM). They would use the LM to land on the Moon.
Maneuvering Thrusters
Forward Hatch
Landing Gear
UNITED STATES
Descent Engine
Ladder

APOLLO 11 LUNAR MODULE (EAGLE)

idea to send an Apollo crew on a journey to the Moon and back—no LM or attempted lunar landing, just a trip around the Moon and then back to Earth in the command and service module (CSM). The command module housed the astronauts, and the service module contained their life-support and fuel equipment. This flight would achieve one of the goals of Apollo, lunar orbit, while development of the LM continued.

Deke Slayton pitched the idea of the new mission to the astronauts. McDivitt and Schweickart opted to stay with *Spider*, but Frank Borman thought the idea of a circumlunar flight intriguing, and he accepted the mission. Thus, he and his crew became the mission known as *Apollo 8*, and McDivitt and his crew became *Apollo 9*.

CHANGES IN BACKUPS

The new mission of *Apollo 8* and the redefinition of McDivitt's crew as *Apollo 9* necessarily led to changes in the backup crews as well. Armstrong, Aldrin, and Haise had been slated as backups to McDivitt, Scott, and Schweickart. With the changes in mission objectives, Armstrong became the backup commander for Borman's new *Apollo 8* mission.

The crew changes meant that Armstrong, Aldrin, and Haise had new goals in their training. Buzz Aldrin, the CSM pilot backup, lent his expertise in celestial navigation to the training regimen, as for the first time, a manned spacecraft would be leaving Earth orbit. The *Apollo 8* astronauts would be faced with new perspectives of the stars they used for navigation, and Aldrin helped them ascertain which stars would be the easiest to see and to use for navigation computation.

Fred Haise, as LM pilot backup, would have no LM piloting for which to train, as the LM would not make the voyage with *Apollo 8*. But he stayed busy with LM simulations and advised the LM development teams at Grumman. Additionally, on *Apollo 8*'s launch date, he worked in the predawn hours to set all the switches in the command module to their preflight configurations.

Armstrong's role as commander had not changed, but since no LM would be flying, Armstrong did not need as much time

As director of NASA's flight crew operations, Deke Slayton assigned astronauts to the Gemini and Apollo missions.

practicing with the LLTV or the LM simulation. But it remained a part of the training regimen.

THE FLIGHT OF *APOLLO 7*

Apollo 8's flight around the Moon was contingent on *Apollo 7* succeeding. The *Apollo 7* mission had several goals. The astronauts would test the *Saturn V* rocket for manned flight, rendezvous with the *Saturn V*'s S-IVB section that would hold the LM, and test the engines on the CSM. Had *Apollo 7*'s tests fallen short of expectations, their goals would have been given to the next mission, and NASA would have pushed all other mission objectives back to succeeding flights.

However, in October 1968, *Apollo 7* accomplished all of its goals. *Apollo 8* was clear to go for its daring mission around the Moon. And during that mission, Neil Armstrong met several times with Deke Slayton to discuss the future.

"YOU'RE IT"

While the *Apollo 8* crew was in space in December 1968, Armstrong and Slayton met to discuss future crew assignments. The astronauts for *Apollo 10* had recently been selected. Slayton asked Armstrong if he would like to command *Apollo 11*, which NASA hoped would be the first to attempt a lunar landing. In later years, speculation arose that NASA offered Armstrong this command because he was a civilian and that NASA chose him because they did not want the Moon landing to look like a military venture. But Slayton believed that Armstrong, among others, would be right for the job. In his memoirs, he wrote: "I had full confidence in Tom Stafford, Neil Armstrong, and Pete Conrad. . . . The system had put them in the right place at the right time. And one of them might very well make the landing."[38]

In addition, Slayton chose to stick with the system of promoting backup crews after a gap of two missions. Thus, he offered the command of *Apollo 11* to Armstrong. He also wanted to promote Michael Collins, who had missed flying on *Apollo 8* because of back surgery, to CSM pilot.

On January 6, 1969, Slayton called Armstrong, Aldrin, and Collins into his office. They received some very thrilling news in the form of two words from Slayton: "You're it."[39] The team that would fly *Apollo 11* was set. Now all they had to do was land on the Moon.

Chapter

6 Training for the Moon

Following his assignment as *Apollo 11* commander in January 1969, Neil Armstrong continued to train for lunar landings in the lunar module (LM) simulators. He and LM pilot Buzz Aldrin studied the complexities of the LM until they knew everything about how it worked. Command and service module (CSM) pilot Michael Collins worked to master the command module, and all three worked to master the intricacies of the flight plan. For some of these challenges, they could depend on the experiences of the *Apollo 8* crew and the other astronauts who were training for later missions. But, in the end, *Apollo 11*'s mission had many challenges that the crew could answer only in space.

CHALLENGES

During the winter of 1969, Armstrong, Aldrin, and Collins knew the challenges they were going to face. Armstrong and Aldrin faced the challenge of maneuvering the LM to a safe landing on the Moon, which had never been done before. They faced the challenge of setting foot on the lunar surface and working in that airless environment, which had also never been

done before. Additionally, they knew that if something went wrong on the surface or in the LM's ascent from the Moon, Michael Collins in the command and service module (CSM) had limited rescue options. They knew that in the worst-case scenarios, such as if the LM crashed on the surface, Collins might have to return to Earth alone. They knew the risks involved.

Also during that winter, many unknown factors were yet to be resolved by other missions. Many years later, Armstrong recalled:

> [T]he lunar module had not flown, hadn't even been in Earth orbit. We didn't know if we could communicate with two vehicles simultaneously at lunar distance. We didn't know whether the radar ranging [system] would work [to determine the LM's altitude above the Moon surface]. A lot of things we just didn't know at that point, and I think that at that point in time I did not really expect that we'd get a chance to try a lunar landing on that flight. Too many things could go wrong on [*Apollo*] 8 or 9 or 10.[40]

Before *Apollo 11* could fly, *Apollo 9* and *Apollo 10* had to achieve their goals. As it turned out, those flights paved the way for the mission of Armstrong, Aldrin, and Collins. *Apollo 11*'s objective of becoming the first to land on the Moon was due to the superb training of the *Apollo 9 and 10* astronauts and the superior performance of the spacecrafts called *Gumdrop, Spider, Charlie Brown,* and *Snoopy.*

SPIDER AND GUMDROP, CHARLIE BROWN AND SNOOPY

After *Apollo 8*'s successful flight in December 1968, Jim McDivitt's crew finally got a chance to try the first fully operational LM in space. In March 1969, *Apollo 9*'s LM, *Spider,* successfully undocked from the CSM, nicknamed *Gumdrop,* and successfully tested the LM's descent rocket, its maneuvering systems, and its ascent engine. McDivitt and LM pilot Rusty Schweickart successfully fired the ascent engine and then made a successful redocking with *Gumdrop.* The mission plan had been ambitious, but *Apollo 9* achieved all its goals.

Now it was *Apollo 10*'s turn. In May, while CSM pilot John Young remained in lunar orbit in the CSM called *Charlie Brown,*

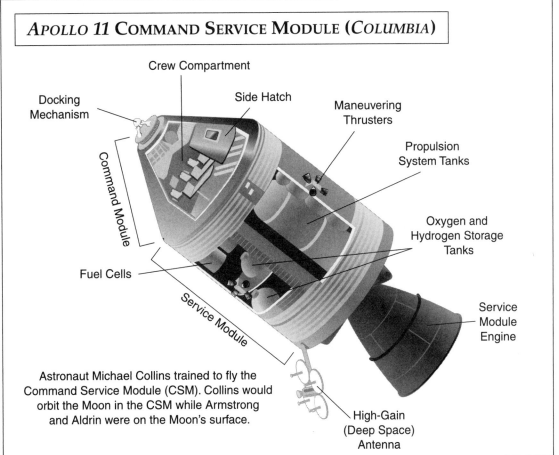

APOLLO 11 COMMAND SERVICE MODULE (COLUMBIA)

Crew Compartment

Docking Mechanism

Side Hatch

Maneuvering Thrusters

Propulsion System Tanks

Command Module

Oxygen and Hydrogen Storage Tanks

Fuel Cells

Service Module

Service Module Engine

Astronaut Michael Collins trained to fly the Command Service Module (CSM). Collins would orbit the Moon in the CSM while Armstrong and Aldrin were on the Moon's surface.

High-Gain (Deep Space) Antenna

Source: NASA

commander Tom Stafford and LM pilot Gene Cernan descended in the LM called *Snoopy* to just fifty thousand feet above the lunar surface. *Snoopy* did not carry enough fuel to make a landing, however; that was for the next flight to try.

Meanwhile, Armstrong, Aldrin, and Collins knew that NASA's next step was to attempt a lunar landing and the extra-vehicular activity (EVA) that would follow it. At the same time, they were aware of the growing interest in their mission and an intense anticipation of the flight among the general public. It was difficult to block out the outside influences, but Armstrong recalled that they "tried to be as focused as we could, work on the things we could do something about, and not worry about the things that were beyond our ability to change."[41]

Saturn V

One of those things that was beyond their ability to change was their launch vehicle: the gigantic *Saturn V* system. The *Saturn V*

A Language All Their Own

As NASA's manned space program became more and more ambitious and technologically complex, a special language evolved, filled with abbreviations, slang, and acronyms. Some are familiar even today, such as LM for lunar module. However, it seemed to Neil Armstrong that the language sometimes got out of hand. In Farmer and Hamblin's book First on the Moon, *he commented on the situation:*

The language of engineering has always been a very precise language. Though a lot of technical words were used, a great effort was usually made to define them clearly so that the audience or the reader should be aware of precisely what had been meant by the statement or by the sentence. We used to make fun of other professions which were less careful with their phraseology and terminology. . . . However, I guess that in recent years [NASA has also had problems, and if] we can't find a word to misuse properly, we'll make one up. An example of misuse is our use of the word *nominal*, which most of the English-speaking world interprets as meaning small, minimal—and we usually use it in the sense of being average or normal. . . .

We can degrade further the usefulness of . . . *nominal* by adding modifiers—for example, *nominalize*, which might be translated into "make standard" or "make normal." And *denominalize* might mean "make abnormal" or "make unusual." This kind of chicanery, when carried to the extreme, might produce such useful words to the English language as "denominalizationmanshipwise."

Technicians stand beside the first stage rocket of the Saturn V. *When fully assembled, the* Saturn V *stood 363 feet tall.*

rocket system was, like the other components of the U.S. space program, a product of the work of many different contractors, specialists, and mechanics. When it was fully assembled, it stood 363 feet tall, longer than a football field. It had thousands of moving parts, valves, pipes, and switches. Armstrong remembered that these parts worked extremely well, substantially better than statistics would have predicted. He attributed this success to the hard work and tremendous dedication of the people who built them, praising the contributions of

> every guy in the project, every guy at the bench building something, every

assembler, every inspector, every guy that's setting up the tests, cranking the torque wrench, and so on, is saying, man or woman, "If anything goes wrong here, it's not going to be my fault, because my part is going to be better than I have to make it." And when you have hundreds of thousands of people all doing their job a little better than they have to, you get an improvement in performance. And that's the only reason we could have pulled this whole thing off.[42]

It was the largest machine ever constructed. The *Saturn V* that was going to launch the *Apollo 11* weighed almost 6.5

million pounds. But that included more than 6 million pounds of fuel. The first stage alone burned fifteen tons of fuel per second for two minutes and forty seconds.

PUBLIC RELATIONS

As impressive as the *Saturn V* system was, it was, after all, just a machine. Even the most casual observers of the space program looked upon it with awe, but much of the attention of both the nation and the world remained focused on the astronauts themselves. After more than six years in the astronaut corps, Armstrong understood that there were certain media demands that astronauts had to meet; they were one of his obligations as part of this elite corps. One of these demands was dealing with *Life* magazine.

From the early days of the Mercury program, NASA had decided to meet the clamoring demands for press interviews and astronaut life stories by setting up an exclusive arrangement with *Life*. The magazine's writers and photographers had almost exclusive access to the astronauts, their training, and their families. The magazine's readers got to see what happened during some of their more adventurous training—such as desert or jungle expeditions, or training for weightlessness in airplanes—and occasionally caught the families in unguarded moments.

For example, during Neil Armstrong's *Gemini VIII* flight, *Life* had a reporter and a photographer in his home. As the flight ran into trouble, the photographer captured Jan seated in front of her TV, anx-

iously awaiting news—and when the crew was reported safe, she slumped over it, relieved, a scene that the photographer also caught on film.

Aware that as the most visible part of the space program they were objects of worldwide interest, the astronauts and their families were gracious about such intentions. Privately, however, they placed a lower priority on public relations than on their missions.

Astronaut training and preparation followed a precise schedule leading toward the launch date. A delay due to something like a rescheduled photography session could jeopardize a launch date.

THE LAUNCH SCHEDULE

The *Apollo 11* launch date was based on very careful calculations. Because the Moon is circling Earth at approximately twenty-three hundred miles an hour, a launch toward the Moon has to take into account not only how long the mission will take to reach it but also where the Moon will be at that time. It is similar to the way a football quarterback throws a pass to a moving receiver. The quarterback needs to anticipate where the receiver will be and how fast the receiver is moving in order to complete the pass. If the quarterback misjudges the receiver's speed or direction, the pass falls incomplete. Unlike the receiver, who can change speed and direction to reach the football, the Moon's direction and speed are constant. Just as a football has no way of redirecting itself toward a receiver, the astronauts had no way to significantly change their course to reach the Moon. Hence the calculations of the Moon's position had to be precise or the astronauts could miss the Moon altogether and hurtle off into space with no chance of returning to Earth.

Additionally, in order to have the right amount of sunlight at the landing site, the scientists needed to calculate the Moon's position relative to the Sun. Furthermore, the scientists needed to choose a suitable area for the landing that was relatively free of craters and boulders and safe for the LM.

All of these calculations led to one day—July 16, 1969—and an optimum lift-off time,

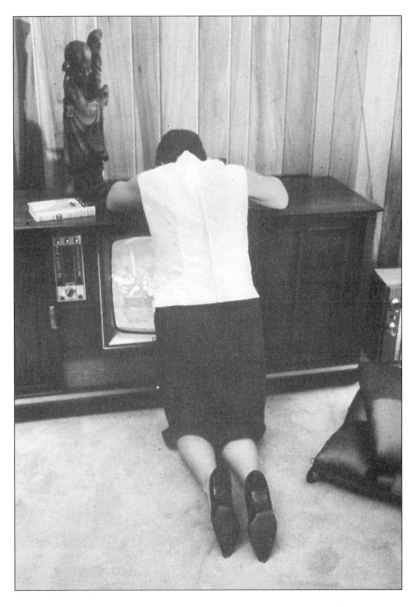

A Life *magazine photographer took this photo of Janet Armstrong slumped over her television, relieved to learn that the crew of* Gemini VIII *had returned to Earth safely.*

9:32 A.M. At that time, the Moon would be in the right place for a flight, and the landing zone—an area of the Moon called the Sea of Tranquility—would have enough lighting for the astronauts to see what they were doing without too much glare. Additionally, the Earth would be in the best position for a suitable reentry and splashdown approximately a week after lift-off.

That meant that a day or even a few hours lost here and there in their training during the spring and early summer of 1969 could lead to an overlooked detail or a poorly understood task. Consequently, the *Apollo 11* astronauts had to budget their time. They worked when they needed to do so until they got something right, saw

their families when they could, and tried to keep focused on the mission's goals. However, on several occasions, something came up that caused concern. Perhaps in hindsight these were insignificant matters, but they deserved attention in order to keep the team on track. One concerned the order in which Aldrin and Armstrong would leave the LM after the landing.

TO BE THE FIRST

Over the years, the debate concerning whether Armstrong or Aldrin would be the first to set foot on the Moon has been discussed far out of proportion to the length

WHAT HAPPENED TO THE SOVIET CHALLENGE

While preparations for the *Apollo 11* launch were under way, the Soviet Union announced plans to send an unmanned craft called *Luna 15* to the Moon. It was to land on the Moon, scoop up a sample of the lunar surface, and then return to Earth. On July 22, 1969, *Luna 15* crashed on the Moon and did not accomplish its goals; in fact, its flight is, in a nutshell, in some ways the story of the Soviet Union's attempts to reach the Moon.

The Soviets faced a number of difficulties. They were hampered by rivalries among competing rocket designers, political rivalries within the Soviet leadership, and ineffective design strategies. Additionally, the death in space of cosmonaut Vladimir Komarov as he returned from orbit in April 1967 set back their manned spacecraft efforts. Their last chance to equal the Americans' success failed in July 1969 when their enormous N-1 rocket, which would have been powerful enough to send a manned mission to the Moon, exploded shortly after take-off.

The Soviet Union's attempts, mishaps, failures, and inadequate planning have been chronicled by many authors. Ultimately, analysts point to the importance of money: the United States invested $25 billion in the Apollo program; the Soviets one-tenth that amount.

Neil Armstrong, Michael Collins, and Buzz Aldrin (left to right) made up the crew of Apollo 11. *As the senior astronaut, Armstrong would step onto the Moon first.*

of time that resolving the problem actually took. The issue developed because Aldrin had noticed in the spring of 1969 that the most recent copies of their flight plan did not specify who would exit first. This puzzled Aldrin; previous editions contained this information. Aldrin wondered if Apollo would continue the tradition of Gemini EVAs, in which the commander stayed in the capsule while the pilot made the space walk. If this trend was continued in the LM, Aldrin would be the first to walk on the Moon.

Then Aldrin began to hear rumors that Armstrong would be the first, solely be-cause he was a civilian. Aldrin hoped to get the issue resolved, so he asked Armstrong how he felt about it:

> I asked him directly, "Neil, you probably know I don't care very much one way or the other about this. But we've got some tough training ahead of us and I think we have to settle this matter before it gets blown out of proportion."

Neil Armstrong was a no-frills kind of guy who didn't talk a whole lot, but usually meant what he said. But there was also a more complex side to Neil, and I think at this point we were both

CRASHING ON "THE MOON"

As Apollo 11's training schedule became more intense, the astronauts almost lived in their simulators. Astronaut Michael Collins, in his book Carrying the Fire, *recalled one failed LM simulated landing and its results:*

Armstrong practices a landing in the lunar module simulator.

Neil and Buzz had been descending in the LM when some catastrophe had overtaken them, and they had been ordered by Houston to abort. Neil, for some reason, either questioned the advice or was just slow to act on it, but in any event, the computer printout showed that the LM had descended below the altitude of the lunar surface before starting to climb again. In plain English, Neil had crashed and destroyed the machine, himself, and Buzz. That night, Buzz was incensed and kept me up far past my bedtime complaining about it. I could not discern whether he was concerned about his actual safety in flight, should Neil repeat this error, or whether he was simply embarrassed to have crashed in front of a roomful of experts in Mission Control in Houston. But no matter, Buzz was in fine voice . . . and [as] his complaints grew louder and more specific, Neil suddenly appeared in his pajamas, tousle-haired and coldly indignant, and joined the fray. Politely I excused myself and gratefully crept off to bed, ... Neil and Buzz continued their discussion far into the night, but the next morning at breakfast neither appeared changed, ruffled, nonplussed, or [angry], so I assume it was a frank and beneficial discussion. . . . It was the only such outburst in our training.

beginning to realize just how important being the first man to set foot on the moon was. Neil hemmed and hawed for a moment and then looked away, breaking eye contact with a coolness I'd never seen in him before. "Buzz," he said, "I realize the historical significance of all this, and I just don't want to rule anything out right now."

I was amazed. We'd become quite friendly during the weeks of our intensified training, but now Neil was distancing himself.[43]

Aldrin contacted George Low, head of the Apollo program in Houston, and asked for a clarification. Low let Deke Slayton deal with it, and one day in April, Slayton called Armstrong and Aldrin together and resolved the issue. Slayton said that Neil Armstrong would be the first man out for two main reasons: First, Armstrong was the senior astronaut of the two; second, the main hatch on the LM was on the left side, where the commander would be. For the LM pilot to be the first out would just be too difficult in a cramped LM with both astronauts wearing bulky spacesuits. Aldrin was disappointed but felt the matter was settled and that the decision had been made with logic and reason.

By now, the training regimen was becoming very tight. July was approaching quickly. The astronauts moved their training to the facilities at Cape Kennedy by the end of May and flew back to Houston on the weekends if they could to see their families. They were almost ready to fly.

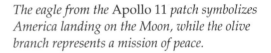

The eagle from the Apollo 11 *patch symbolizes America landing on the Moon, while the olive branch represents a mission of peace.*

But Armstrong, Aldrin, and Collins had many other matters on their minds. Some concerned the overall mission; others concerned smaller, more personal details.

DETAILS, DETAILS

By the end of May, they were spending up to fourteen hours a day in the simulators, playing out "what if?" scenarios, trying to determine if they were missing any small detail. They saw their families rarely, and Jan Armstrong was very concerned: She said,

He used to come home with his face drawn white, and I was worried about him. I was worried about all of them. The worst period was in early June. Their morale was down. They were worried about whether there was time enough for them to learn the things they had to learn, to do the things they had to do, if this mission was to work. [44]

One of the details concerned the names they were going to give the CSM and the LM. Collins, who was the crew artist, sketched out a number of ideas for their mission patch that they hoped would reflect their peaceful mission. Armstrong remembered that they had received many suggestions from NASA staff and from the general public. They liked the idea of using an olive branch in the design, which had been suggested by one of the simulator engineers in Houston, as it suggested their mission of peace. Eventually, they added an American bald eagle, to symbolize the nation, landing on the Moon clutching the olive branch.

That led the astronauts to name the LM *Eagle;* they felt that it reflected both the theme of the patch and their national pride in the mission. From there, they decided on *Columbia* for the CSM; Armstrong said that the choice "was an attempt to reflect the sense of adventure and exploration and seriousness with which Columbus undertook his assignment in 1492." [45]

The crew unveiled their patch and the nicknames for the LM and CSM during their final press conference in Houston on Saturday, July 5. It was also their final weekend with their families; after the Fourth of July weekend, they would be at Cape Kennedy full time. The scheduled launch date was now only eleven days away.

7 A Dream Come True

In the second week of July 1969, it seemed that *Apollo 11* was ready to fly on schedule. Neil Armstrong, Buzz Aldrin, and Michael Collins felt that they were fully prepared to go. Now all they needed was the same assessment from NASA officials.

GO FOR LAUNCH

On July 12, one week after the astronauts unveiled their mission patch and their spacecrafts' nicknames, Deke Slayton, the medical personnel, and the heads of NASA held a conference call to discuss the launch. All felt that the mission was, in NASA slang, a "go." The countdown would proceed as scheduled, with lift-off still set for 9:32 A.M. on July 16. The decision excited the astronauts. Jan remembered, "When I talked to Neil on the Monday [of launch week, two days before lift-off] he was ready to go. When I talked to him on Tuesday he was *really* ready. They were ready to go *then*." [46]

Finally, July 16 arrived. Deke Slayton woke the astronauts in the crew quarters at Cape Kennedy at 4:15 A.M., and they went through a final medical checkup before having breakfast. At 5:55 A.M. they started suiting up for their flight. The as-

tronauts rode up in the elevator and climbed into *Columbia*. Backup lunar module (LM) pilot Fred Haise helped them secure their hose lines and strapped them into their seats. They were right on schedule when Haise exited, closed, and sealed the hatch at 7:52 A.M.

As the astronauts went through their series of prelaunch checks, the countdown continued smoothly toward 9:32. Precisely as scheduled, the *Saturn V*'s huge first-stage engines roared to life, and *Apollo 11* was on its way.

Jan Armstrong and her two sons—Ricky, now twelve, and Mark, now six—were watching the launch from a friend's yacht anchored in Florida's Banana River, not far from the launch complex. When lift-off came, they could hear it on the radio, but they could not locate it in the sky. Then Jan located it as the first stage dropped away and exclaimed, "There it is!" [47] Now that the launch was completed, she would have to follow the rest of the mission as millions of others would: at home, on radio, and on television.

APOLLO APPROACHES THE MOON

Over the next three days, television and radio broadcasts tracked *Apollo 11* as it crossed the gulf from Earth to the Moon. On Friday, July 18, the astronauts broadcast a live television show from the spacecraft, which Jan, her mother, her sisters and their husbands, and Ricky and Mark watched with great interest.

By the end of the ninety-minute broadcast, *Apollo 11* had traveled over 2,000 miles farther from Earth and was more than 175,000 miles from home. The flight was fifty-seven hours old, and the astronauts were traveling in the gulf of space between Earth and the Moon, with Earth's gravity diminishing its influence on the spacecraft. But within the next six hours, the Moon's gravity started drawing *Apollo 11* closer, and

Armstrong, Collins, and Aldrin (front to rear) smile and wave as they walk to the Apollo 11 *launchpad on July 16, 1969.*

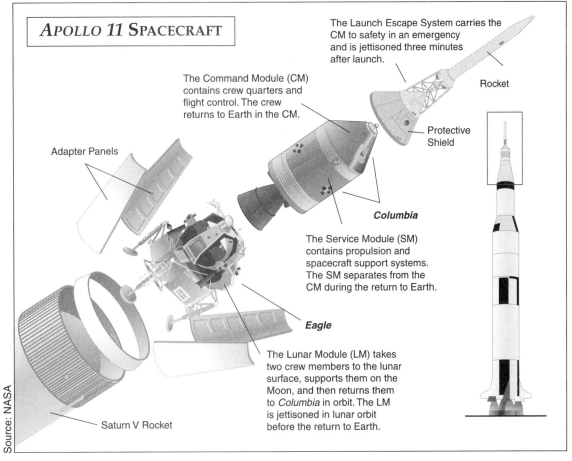

APOLLO 11 SPACECRAFT

The Launch Escape System carries the CM to safety in an emergency and is jettisoned three minutes after launch.

Rocket

The Command Module (CM) contains crew quarters and flight control. The crew returns to Earth in the CM.

Protective Shield

Adapter Panels

Columbia

The Service Module (SM) contains propulsion and spacecraft support systems. The SM separates from the CM during the return to Earth.

Eagle

The Lunar Module (LM) takes two crew members to the lunar surface, supports them on the Moon, and then returns them to *Columbia* in orbit. The LM is jettisoned in lunar orbit before the return to Earth.

Saturn V Rocket

they were now traveling about twenty-six hundred miles an hour.

LUNAR ORBIT

By Saturday, July 19, the mission was seventy-five hours old, and *Apollo 11* was preparing to go into lunar orbit. The decision to do so was Armstrong's alone, as he had to make it when the spacecraft was on the far side of the Moon and therefore out of communication with Houston. But the important orbital "burn" of the command and service module (CSM) engine was

completed without a hitch. The crew was one step closer to attempting a landing.

They made twelve more orbits before the time came to separate the lunar module (LM) from the CSM. Armstrong and Aldrin climbed into the LM and started enabling its systems, turning on the computer and testing *Eagle*'s communications with Houston. Once the LM was fully functioning, Armstrong and Aldrin returned to the CSM and started putting on their pressure suits; there would be no room to do so in the LM. It was early Sunday morning, July 20, in Houston.

Next, Armstrong and Aldrin prepared to separate from the CSM and perform a deorbital burn (a carefully timed firing of the LM's descent engine), which would send the LM toward the lunar surface while the CSM stayed in orbit. The Houston technicians could tell that the undocking had occurred, but they wanted to hear how the astronauts felt about it. Armstrong replied, "The *Eagle* has wings."[48] They were on their way to the lunar surface.

"PROGRAM ALARM"

As Armstrong and Aldrin descended toward the lunar surface, they encountered problems communicating with Houston. Collins, alone in orbit in *Columbia,* relayed a suggestion from Houston for the LM to adjust its attitude slightly. It worked. Shortly thereafter, Armstrong and Aldrin were given the go for a program called powered descent, in which the LM's engine fired to slow its orbit and bring it closer to the lunar surface.

As they descended through 40,000 feet above the surface, the LM's landing radar came on. It fed information to the LM's computer, which automatically revised the craft's trajectory with bursts from the maneuvering jets. Armstrong was surprised at hearing them so often; the simulators' jets had not been this busy.

Aldrin kept a close watch on the computer displays, reading out the figures so that both Armstrong and Houston could hear them. Suddenly, the astronauts heard the high-pitched buzz of the master alarm signal. The display's program light glowed. Armstrong announced, "Program alarm." Author Andrew Chaikin describes the next tension-filled moments:

Quickly, Aldrin queried the computer for the alarm code, and "1202" flashed on the display. Aldrin did not know just what a 1202 meant—and this was not the time to dig out the data book to find out—but it had something to do with the computer being overloaded with too many things to do.[49]

Computer experts in Houston soon advised that the 1202 program alarm had been activated because the LM's computer was was receiving more information from the landing radar and other equipment than it could handle. It was trying to halt all its computations and restart. The problem remained intermittent, which did not interfere with the descent, but that first program alarm had prevented Armstrong from surveying the landscape outside his window as scheduled, to check where the computer was pointing the LM. At 7,500 feet above the surface, the *Eagle* pitched forward, and the astronauts got their first good look at their landing zone. Armstrong did not like what he saw.

TAKING CONTROL

Armstrong discovered that not only did they seem to be headed for an automatic landing beyond the original destination, but they also seemed to be heading toward a boulder field. He took control of the landing cycle, switching to attitude-hold mode, which let the descent rocket brake the LM's fall without slowing its horizontal flight.

Aldrin concentrated on reading off the critical numbers to Armstrong—their rate of descent, their forward motion, and their altitude. In Houston, the control room went silent; they knew nothing of the boulder field and were hearing only Aldrin's numbers.

The LM passed below 300 feet and flew over a crater, and Armstrong found that the first site he had picked out was no good. Time was critical now: they needed to save at least twenty seconds of the descent engine's fuel for a possible emergency return to *Columbia*. With only ninety seconds of fuel remaining in the descent engine's supply, Armstrong selected an area of about 200 square feet as his target. He tried to focus on the landing area and to bring the LM straight down, but the descent engine was kicking up more dust than expected. However, the LM was descending no faster than an elevator, and Armstrong brought it down gently and safely to a landing on the Moon. He had had a mere twenty seconds of fuel remaining.

REACTIONS

Radio and television stations broadcast the news of the landing. Millions of people around the world breathed sighs of relief or were moved to tears. Collins radioed down that "It sure sounded great from up here. You guys did a fantastic job."[50]

Neil Armstrong (left) and Buzz Aldrin (right) took these photos of each other in the Eagle, *the lunar module. At the time the photos were taken, the two had already completed their moon walk.*

On the Moon's surface, Armstrong and Aldrin grinned at each other and shook hands on their achievement. Author Andrew Chaikin called the landing "everything that a pilot could ask for."[51] It had presented Armstrong the challenge of a lifetime: piloting an untested vehicle to a landing in unknown terrain. But for all the challenges this had posed to Armstrong the test pilot, it had also marked a stunning achievement for Armstrong the engineer. He had contributed to the development of equipment that had navigated a hostile environment. Additionally, he had mastered the technology that had taken him there and enabled him to achieve the lunar landing.

However, he had little time to marvel over this achievement. The astronauts' flight plan was far too busy. Armstrong and Aldrin moved on to their next task.

TRANQUILITY BASE

With the LM safely on the Moon, Armstrong had a chance to look around at the landscape of the landing site, which, because they had landed in the Sea of Tranquility, he had called Tranquility Base. He remembered years later that he was "surprised by the apparent closeness of the horizon," and how the lunar dust settled after they shut off the LM's engine:

I was absolutely dumbfounded when I shut the rocket engine off and the particles that were going out radially from the bottom of the engine fell all the way out over the horizon, and when I shut the engine off, they just raced out over the horizon and instantaneously dis-

appeared, you know, just like it had been shut off for a week. That was remarkable. I'd never seen that. I'd never seen anything like that. And logic says, yes, that's the way it ought to be there, but I hadn't thought about it and I was surprised.[52]

No one was surprised, however, by the astronauts' eagerness to begin the EVA as soon as possible. The astronauts had a meal and began the arduous task of putting on their spacesuits for the EVA. It took longer than expected, but they could not afford to rush. The suits contained everything they needed for survival on the airless surface of the Moon: oxygen, drinking water, and a temperature control unit to keep them warm in the shade and cool in the sun.

Finally, around 10:30 P.M. eastern time, they began to open the 42-inch-square hatch of the LM. Once it was open, Armstrong started to crawl through the opening, feet first, facedown. Armstrong worked his way down the ladder, pulled a lever that released and activated a TV camera on the outside of the LM, and, as the world watched, jumped 3 feet down to the footpad of the LM. Testing his ability to work in the reduced gravity of the Moon, he jumped up and then down. He commented on the Moon's appearance and then said, "I'm going to step off the LM now."[53]

At 10:56 P.M. eastern time, Neil Armstrong became the first human being to set foot on the surface of the Moon. He said, simply, "That's one small step for (a) man, one giant leap for mankind."[54] Fourteen minutes later, Aldrin joined him. As Aldrin climbed down, he admired the view, but

"That's One Small Step . . ."

Although millions of people heard and saw Neil Armstrong when he first set foot on the Moon, there is some debate over what *exactly he said. On the thirtieth anniversary of the landing, Armstrong helped set the record straight. In "One Small Step for a Man? Even Armstrong Isn't Sure It's 'a' or Nay" the Associated Press gives this account:*

Armstrong's first steps and his first words spoken on the Moon were televised around the world.

He thought he said it. He meant to say it. But 30 years after he blasted off on *Apollo 11*, Neil Armstrong can't be certain he inserted an "a" before "man" in his moon-stepping speech.

"That's one small step for man, one giant leap for mankind," is how history has recorded the first words uttered by the first man to tread the lunar surface.

In his first news conference in years, . . . Armstrong said "After landing, actually having been somewhat surprised, the fact that we were able to make a successful touchdown, I realized I was going to have to say something. . . . "

"But it wasn't anything very complicated. When you just think about stepping off, why, it seemed to follow."

What didn't follow, at least for those listening back on Earth, was "a"—the subject of decades of debate among space historians and space buffs. Armstrong speculated after the mission that his voice-operated transmitter may not have picked up the word.

"The 'a' was intended," Armstrong explained to reporters. "I thought I said it. I can't hear it when I listen on the radio reception here on Earth. So I'll be happy if you just put it in parentheses."

his powers of description seemed to be lost for a moment. He said, simply, "Beautiful view." Armstrong replied, "Isn't that something? Magnificent sight out here," and suddenly Aldrin had the words for which he had been searching. With a sense of wonder in his voice, he said, quietly, "Magnificent desolation."[55]

MEN ON THE MOON

Over the next two-and-a-half hours, the two astronauts kept busy with the tasks on their checklist. They moved the TV camera to a stand away from the LM so everyone could watch their activities. They set up several experiments for scientists on Earth to watch, such as a seismograph that would relay the occurrence of any lunar earthquakes back to Earth. They collected samples of Moon rock and dust for geologists to examine, and they took close-up photographs of the lunar surface.

They also unveiled a special plaque that would remain on the Moon's surface. The plaque had images of Earth's two hemispheres, the names and signatures of the

Armstrong snapped this photo of Buzz Aldrin standing on the lunar surface. The landing gear of the lunar module can be seen in the background.

"MUSIC OUT OF THE MOON"

Each astronaut on the Apollo flights was allowed a small number of personal possessions that he stashed in a personal preferences kit. During Apollo 11, *Neil Armstrong decided to take along a tape recording of some music that he and Jan especially liked. In* First on the Moon, Gene Farmer and Dora Jane Hamblin *note why it was special:*

Some years earlier, Neil had fallen in love with a recording by Samuel Hoffman called *Music out of the Moon*. One of the principal instruments used in making the recording was the theremin. . . . [I]t generated tones electronically, controlled by the distance between the musician's hands and two metal rods which served as antennas. When Neil was flying experimental aircraft at Edwards, Jan used to listen to this record by the hour at their home in the California mountains. It was one of the many things that was destroyed by fire in 1964, and before. . . . *Apollo 11* . . . Neil asked that a search be made for the record: "Somebody found it and taped it. I don't even know who it was." He did know that he wanted to play it back to earth.

After he got home, [Jan] asked, "Where on earth did you find that? We used to listen to that all the time."

Apollo 11 crew and President Richard M. Nixon, and the inscription, "Here Men From Planet Earth First Set Foot Upon the Moon. July 1969 A.D. We Came In Peace For All Mankind." [56]

Then they set up a U.S. flag. Since there is no atmosphere on the Moon, a regular flag would sit limply against the flagpole. But this one was specially made, with a stiffening rod at its top edge, so that the flag would stand out straight from the pole. Armstrong took a photograph of Aldrin next to the flag with the LM in the background; it seemed to encapsulate the nation's achievements in fulfilling President Kennedy's challenge in 1961.

Soon, Houston started radioing warnings that it was time to return to the LM. The astronauts had accomplished as much as they could in the time they had been allotted, but they had wanted to do much more. Armstrong said many years later that he hadn't done as good a job as he would have liked in gathering the rock samples.

It was at the end of our [time] period on the surface . . . we were running low on time, and the geologists . . . would have liked us to authenticate each sample with photographs from different directions. . . . I thought, since we didn't have time to do it, the better part of

ISOLATION

Because of the possibility that Armstrong, Aldrin, and Collins might return from the Moon with some form of contagion unknown to Earth scientists, NASA took the precaution of isolating the astronauts from the outside world in the LRL. Andrew Chaikin, in his book A Man on the Moon, *described the crew's reaction to the isolation:*

For the next two weeks [after they returned to Houston] they lived within the Lunar Receiving Laboratory, recounting all aspects of the flight in minute detail. . . . As the days passed, the men joked about being jailed, and at the close of one of the debriefing sessions they called out to the engineers on the other side of the glass, "You know where to find us! We're not going anywhere!" In the off hours, there were movies . . . and card games. . . . And though the LRL wasn't a bad place— it had a bar, and an exercise room—time dragged. At the end of one debriefing, when asked, "Any other comments?" Collins said quietly, "I want out."

valor was to just pick up all the different kinds of samples as I could, stick them in the bag and get them back in the [LM].[57]

Armstrong and Aldrin returned to the LM and secured the hatch a bit after 1 A.M. eastern time, July 21. Their time on the Moon surface was almost over.

RETURNING HOME

Armstrong and Aldrin took care of a number of post-EVA chores, stowed equipment, and answered myriad questions from Houston before finally getting some rest. They had been awake for almost twenty-two hours, but they slept fitfully; the LM itself was small and cramped, and the interior was uncomfortably cold. And the events of the EVA and the upcoming lift-off were playing through their minds.

When Houston gave them a wake-up call later that Monday morning, July 21, they were ready to get to work. They made final preparations for lift-off. At 1:54 P.M., the ascent engine lit, and they made a smooth trip into orbit. Jan Armstrong had been worrying about this part of the mission, perhaps, most of all. She was worried that Neil and Buzz might be stranded on the Moon's surface. She said she knew that as long as the ascent engine fired and that as long as they got off the surface, "Mike will come and get them, wherever they are. Wherever they are, he would come. Nobody [at NASA] told me that. Nobody ever had to. He would."[58]

Collins did not need to make any emergency rescue maneuvers, as *Eagle* flew up to meet *Columbia* precisely as planned. With the redocking, all three *Apollo 11* astronauts were together again. Armstrong and Aldrin climbed back into the CSM, transferring their boxes of Moon samples to the command module and stowing unneeded gear in the ascent stage of the LM, which they then jettisoned. Then they got ready for the trip back to Earth. They made a burn to leave the lunar orbit, and when capsule commander Charlie Duke asked, "How did it go?" Armstrong replied, "Tell them to open up the LRL [lunar receiving laboratory] doors, Charlie."[59] They were headed home.

SPLASHDOWN AND CELEBRATION

The LRL was a sealed three-story building at the Manned Space Center in Houston that was set to house the astronauts when they returned to Earth. No one was exactly sure what working in the lunar environment would do to the astronauts, so they would be housed in the LRL for two weeks to ensure they had no extraterrestrial contaminations.

On board the aircraft carrier USS *Hornet*, the recovery ship for *Apollo 11*, preparations for the astronauts' isolation were also complete by the time Armstrong radioed that they were headed home. *Columbia* splashed down in the Pacific Ocean on Thursday, July 24, and President Nixon greeted the astronauts on board the *Hor-*

net. Back in Houston, the crew's wives faced the media. Jan Armstrong found that the only way she could describe the flight was that "it was out of this world," adding heartfelt thanks to "all of NASA, to all the contractors who have helped to make this flight successful, to the astronaut crew, to the three men . . . and to all the people of the world, we thank them for everything. . . . Their prayers, their thoughts, just everything."[60]

Meanwhile, the *Hornet* steamed for Hawaii, arriving three days later; the astronauts, housed in a sealed, modified travel trailer called the mobile quarantine facility, were then flown to Houston and ushered into the LRL. They were finally released on August 11 with a clean bill of health and reunited with their families. Michael Collins wrote that they emerged into a warm Houston night to a warm welcome: "[I] get my first smell of the earth in nearly a month—warm and moist and inviting and reassuring. I don't recall being sensitive to earth smells before, but then perhaps my sensitivities have changed and I will find the earth a different place from now on."[61]

Indeed, each astronaut found Earth a different place. And each was now faced with a decision about what to do after *Apollo 11*.

8 Retreating from the Spotlight

On August 13, 1969, two days after releasing the astronauts from the LRL, NASA sent Armstrong, Collins, and Aldrin on a one-day publicity tour of New York, Chicago, and Los Angeles. They rode in ticker-tape parades in each city; in New York, throngs of well-wishers tried to swarm the motorcade. At the end of the long day, President Nixon hosted the three men at a gala reception in Los Angeles.

NASA kept finding official functions for the *Apollo 11* astronauts to perform as a crew. In addition to having them address a joint session of Congress in the fall of 1969, NASA sent them on a round-the-world goodwill trip, starting in late September. It was a whirlwind affair—twenty-eight cities in thirty-eight days. But after the intense preparations for and the achievements of the *Apollo 11* flight, everything seemed a bit anticlimactic. A reception on the White House lawn after the trip ended seemed even more mundane. President Nixon asked if any of the astronauts would enjoy being ambassadors; each turned him down. Now it was time for each to consider life after *Apollo 11*. For Neil Armstrong, that meant a return to Houston—for the time being.

LIFE AFTER THE MOON

Shortly after the hubbub of the *Apollo 11* flight died down, the *Apollo 11* astronauts went their separate ways. Mike Collins resigned from NASA and became assistant secretary of state for public affairs in Washington, D.C. Buzz Aldrin moved from the active astronaut corps to the development program that was working on the fledgling design that eventually became the space shuttle. Neil Armstrong returned to the Astronaut Office, hoping that some day he might fly in space again. But instead of putting a very famous astronaut back into the flight rotation, NASA officials offered Armstrong a position as deputy associate administrator of aeronautics. Armstrong accepted the position, and in early 1970, the Armstrong family left El Lago, Texas, where they had lived since 1962.

Armstrong's new job was at NASA headquarters office in Washington, D.C. He soon discovered that Washington was not the place for him. It seemed that NASA wanted him in Washington, not as an engineer and a pilot, but as the *Apollo 11* commander whom the agency could send to myriad social functions. He found the essentially political position both enlightening and frustrating:

[Washington, D.C. is] a frustrating place for me because so much coordination and greasing the skids [that is, promising favors] goes on in Washington that by the time you've gotten around to everybody, the first guy's forgotten what the subject was. It's really hard to get things done there, and it's amazing to me that anybody can get things rolling from Washington, just because of the nature of the place.[62]

After fewer than two years in the Washington office, Armstrong decided he had had enough. He began exploring other options and started reexamining some of his goals in life. According to Andrew Chaikin, "In 1962, he had mentioned to the other astronauts that he planned to write an engineering textbook some day."[63] Now, at age forty-one, he decided to pursue a new career that might lead to that engineering textbook. He decided that he wanted to teach.

The Apollo 11 *astronauts wave to the crowd during a parade held in their honor in New York. The crew was honored at official functions throughout 1969.*

Leaving NASA, Returning to Ohio

On September 24, 1971, Neil Armstrong resigned from NASA. Including his time with NASA's predecessor, the NACA, he had worked for the agency since 1955. But now he certainly had a new challenge ahead of him. He had accepted a teaching position in his home state of Ohio at the University of Cincinnati. He told a NASA historian that he expected to work on his writing skills (he confessed, "I don't write very well") and intended to do some studying there as well as teaching, in order to make himself a "better teacher."[64]

His first day as a teacher in the engineering department turned out to be filled with unexpected distractions. According to Kathy Sawyer of the *Washington Post*,

Armstrong's first day as a professor attracted reporters and photographers to the engineering building. Once his 18 students were inside the classroom and the clock ticked past 2 P.M. he slammed the door shut. "He was pretty nervous

APOLLO PROGRAM–MANNED MISSIONS
OCTOBER 1968 TO DECEMBER 1972

Flight	Crew	Launch Date
Apollo 1	Ed White, Gus Grissom, Roger Chaffee	*
Apollo 7	Wally Schirra, Donn Eisele, Duke Cunningham	October 1968
Apollo 8	Frank Borman, Jim Lovell, William Anders	December 1968
Apollo 9	Jim McDivitt, Dave Scott, Rusty Schweickart	March 1969
Apollo 10	Tom Stafford, John Young, Gene Cernan	May 1969
Apollo 11	Neil Armstrong, Michael Collins, Buzz Aldrin	July 1969
Apollo 12	Pete Conrad, Richard Gordon, Alan Bean	November 1969
Apollo 13	Jim Lovell, John Swigert, Fred Haise	April 1970
Apollo 14	Alan Shepard, Stuart Roosa, Edgar Mitchell	January 1971
Apollo 15	Dave Scott, Alfred Worden, James Irwin	July 1971
Apollo 16	John Young, Thomas Mattingly, Charles Duke	April 1972
Apollo 17	Gene Cernan, Ronald Evans, Harrison Schmitt	December 1972

* Apollo 1 was destroyed January 1967 during a preflight test. All three astronauts were killed.

Source: NASA

. . . but that was only natural," recalls Dave Burrus, then a third-year engineering student. "When the class was over, the hall had filled up with reporters. . . . (Armstrong) had his hand on the doorknob and he pushed us out as fast as possible, and slammed the door shut again."[65]

Eventually, the campus grew accustomed to his presence, although the university police had to establish what one official called buffers around Armstrong to allow him to get his work done.

Although Armstrong was now a university professor and no longer an astronaut, his fame had not diminished. Over the next several years, journalists, the public, and companies continued to seek Armstrong out for interviews, appearances, and endorsements. Dozens of universities and colleges wished to confer honorary degrees upon him, if he would speak at comencements or other ceremonies. The University of Cincinnati understood Armstrong's reluctance to participate in most of these events and ensured that its own faculty and staff respected his wishes. He had differences with the university people on other issues, however, and he abruptly resigned from his position on New Year's Day, 1980.

Nevertheless, Armstrong describes his time at the university as worthwhile:

I spent nearly a decade there teaching engineering. I really enjoyed it. I love to teach. I love the kids, only they were smarter than I was, which made it a challenge.

But I found the governance unexpectedly difficult, and I was poorly prepared and trained to handle some of the aspects, not the teaching, but . . . universities operate differently than the world I came from . . . actually, I stayed in that job longer than any job I'd ever had up to that point, but I decided it was time for me to go on and try some other things.[66]

MOVING ON

One of the other things Armstrong wanted to try was farming. He and Jan had purchased a 200-acre dairy farm in Lebanon, Ohio, about thirty miles from Cincinnati, in 1971. After he resigned from the university, he spent much more time on the farm.

One of Armstrong's longtime friends, Robert Hotz, understands Armstrong's attraction to the land. A former editor of *Aviation Week* magazine and a farmer in rural Maryland, Hotz says that once out on the farm, a person starts to gain perspective.

Hotz commented that compared to things like hills and mountains, "You understand that you're a short-term phenomenon, like the mosquitoes that come in the spring and the fall. You get a perspective on yourself. You're getting back to the fundamentals of the planet. Neil feels that way, because we've talked about it, and so do I."[67]

The farm allowed Armstrong a sense of space, space to work, and space away from the demands of celebrity. Residents of Lebanon would occasionally spot him driving around town, stopping at the feed

Aldrin, Collins, and Armstrong (left to right) inspect a two-pound rock they brought back from the Moon. The rock is now on display at the Smithsonian.

store, the ice cream parlor, or the historic hotel with its fine restaurant. But for the most part, they left him alone, which was fine with Armstrong. He said, "I don't want to be a living memorial." [68]

SERVING HIS COUNTRY ONCE AGAIN

In addition to his work on the farm, Armstrong became involved with private in-

dustry. Starting in the 1980s, he served on the boards of several engineering and defense contracting firms. Then in 1986, following the explosion of the space shuttle *Challenger,* he was asked to serve on a presidential commission that would investigate the disaster. President Ronald Reagan selected former Secretary of State William P. Rogers to lead the investigation and asked Armstrong to be the vice chairman.

Armstrong and the retired diplomat worked very well together, and the commission's report led to improvements in space shuttle equipment and the conditions under which it could be launched.

Serving on the commission brought Armstrong into contact with the firms that served as contractors to the space program in particular and the U.S. government in general. These contacts led him into the next phase of his post-NASA career.

CORPORATE POSITIONS

Armstrong found that several of the firms that were contracting for the space shuttle program were interested in enlisting his engineering expertise. After the *Challenger* commission, he served on the board of Cordant Technologies, Inc., which produces the solid-rocket boosters for the space shuttle. He also served as the chairman of the board

THE NEIL ARMSTRONG AIR & SPACE MUSEUM

Tucked away on an inside page of the *New York Times* on July 22, 1969, a one-sentence article noted that Ohio governor James A. Rhodes announced plans to raise $1 million for a Neil Armstrong museum, even though the *Apollo 11* flight had not yet ended. Today, the Neil Armstrong Air & Space Museum in Wapakoneta, Ohio, is a part of the Ohio Historical Society. The museum's website says the museum documents "Ohio's contributions to space flight," boasts Armstrong's *Gemini VIII* capsule, as well as artifacts from *Apollo 11* and a Moon rock.

The museum helps keep the contributions of Armstrong and other Ohioans associated with space flight alive, but Armstrong himself has no association with the museum. Marcia Dunn of the Associated Press, in the article "Neil Armstrong, 30 Years Later: Still Reticent After All These Years," says that the museum has become the recipient of requests for Armstrong's attention:

> We just are bombarded weekly with requests for him, everything from "Will you sign this for me?" to "Will you come to my son's Boy Scout, Eagle Scout program?" said museum manager John Zwez.
>
> Zwez wishes Armstrong, who has an office in Lebanon, Ohio, would drop by now and then and mingle with visitors. Armstrong has no ties to the 27-year-old museum and has been there only five or six times.
>
> "On the other hand," Zwez noted, "the fact that Neil Armstrong is quiet and reserved about the whole thing perhaps is the better approach than going out there and selling this and selling that, promoting this and promoting that."

of AIL Systems, a defense electronics company in New York, from 1989 to 2000. In 2000, AIL merged with EDO Corporation of California, which specializes in engineering, electronic warfare, and information technology solutions; Armstrong joined the EDO board of directors following the merger. On May 7, 2002, he retired as chairman of the board of EDO.

Although Armstrong has retired, he still stays involved in various activities, such as public speaking and educating groups about engineering and the space program. He still holds a private pilot's license and continues to enjoy flying as much as ever. And, ever the private individual, he carefully picks when and where to make public appearances.

INFREQUENT BUT MEMORABLE APPEARANCES

Each of the public events that Armstrong chooses to attend, and each of the speeches he chooses to make, must meet his own criteria of importance. He does not regularly attend NASA anniversary celebrations; for example, in 1994, he did not attend the official twenty-fifth anniversary ceremonies of the *Apollo 11* landing, but he did make a number of appearances in connection with the thirtieth anniversary in 1999.

In 2001, Armstrong agreed to participate in NASA's Oral History Project, and on September 19, he sat down with authors Stephen E. Ambrose and Douglas Brinkley and several NASA historians at the Johnson Space Center in Houston. He answered a wide range of questions about the history

of NASA, his role in the manned space program, his life since NASA, and about the future of manned space flight. The participants speculated about a manned trip to Mars, and Armstrong quipped, "If they offered me command of a Mars mission, I'd jump at it." [69] A year earlier, in 2000, at a National Press Club luncheon, Armstrong was asked about sending humans to Mars; he replied, "Well, uh, I'd volunteer," drawing laughter and applause. [70]

Even with these appearances, he admitted during the Oral History Project interview that he is still bombarded with requests for interviews and endorsements and that he cannot agree to them all. As an example, Armstrong pointed out that he has received numerous invitations to receive honorary degrees. He joked that it was not very difficult to turn down Harvard University, but, "It's very difficult to turn down Sister Frances Marie [Thrailkill, College of Mount St. Joseph, Cincinnati, Ohio]." [71]

PRIVATE MATTERS REMAIN PRIVATE

Perhaps at least partly because Armstrong has limited his post-Apollo forays into the limelight, his public image remains almost as untarnished as it was during the halcyon days of the lunar project. Few casual followers of the space program are aware that Armstrong had a heart attack in 1991, from which he has fully recovered. And few people know that he and Jan quietly divorced in 1994. At their mutual request, the judge temporarily sealed the proceedings,

Armstrong has led a quiet life since walking on the Moon. The public remained unaware that he and Jan had divorced until this photo depicting him with his second wife, Carol Knight, appeared in early 2003.

which meant the divorce attracted little attention in the media. Shortly thereafter, Armstrong remarried; his new wife, Carol Knight, is fifteen years younger than he, and is a woman whom her friends describe as chatty and very friendly. In fact, this second marriage is so little known that a photograph of Neil and Carol, taken by the Reuters news agency in 2003, identified her as Janet Armstrong.

Armstrong's post-NASA life is not unlike that of some of his colleagues. Of his

ARMSTRONG ASSESSES THE SPACE PROGRAM— PAST, PRESENT, AND FUTURE

In an oral history interview for NASA at the Johnson Space Center in September 2001, Armstrong expressed an opinion about why he thought the manned space program had declined in popularity and in achievements since the Apollo program. He said that part of it had to do with the United States redirecting budgetary funding to more pressing concerns, such as environmental problems. In addition, he felt that it also had to do with short attention spans:

Oh, I think it's predominantly the responsibility of the human character. We don't have a very long attention span, and needs and pressures vary from day to day, and we have a difficult time remembering a few months ago, or we have a difficult time looking very far into the future. We're very "now" oriented. I'm not surprised by that. I think we'll always be in space, but it will take us longer to do the new things than the advocates would like, and in some cases it will take external factors or forces which we can't control and can't anticipate that will cause things to happen or not happen. Nevertheless, looking back, we were really very privileged to live in that thin slice of history where we changed how man looks at himself and what he might become and where he might go. So I'm very thankful that we got to see that and be part of it.

fellow New Nine astronauts from 1962 and their wives, only two couples—Jim and Marilyn Lovell and Frank and Linda Borman—remain married. Other former astronauts, such as Buzz Aldrin, have had difficulty dealing with the post-NASA world; Aldrin is candid about the bouts of alcoholism and depression with which he struggled after he left Houston.

But Armstrong left NASA with a fairly clear idea of what he wanted to do. He wanted to return to engineering. At a sold-out speech to the National Press Club in 2000, he said, "I am, and ever will be, a white socks, pocket protector nerdy engineer. And I take a substantial amount of pride in the accomplishments of my profession."[72]

Armstrong continues to see himself as part of the community of engineers and as one who has made some contributions to the field. But he refuses to allow himself to be continually singled out within the engineering community merely because he was an astronaut. However, he is famous for that part of his life. Because it remains in the public eye, he has retreated from the spotlight in order to move on with his life and his other interests.

Many of Armstrong's colleagues understand his motives. The late Pete Conrad, who commanded *Apollo 12,* once said,

"Neil's entitled to do his thing," and his crewmate Dick Gordon commented that although Armstrong certainly has the capability of telling his story whenever requested, "He chooses not to. You can imagine what would happen if he started something like that. I mean, the poor guy would never have any peace of mind."[73] These opinions among those who knew Armstrong before and during the height of the Apollo program reflect an understanding of Armstrong's character: He is a talented engineer and an outstanding pilot but also a reserved, soft-spoken, and private person. These have been his hallmarks for more than fifty years. They are the reason Neil Armstrong remains as important today as when he first became a household name and why he will remain an important individual in history, no matter what the future holds.

THE FUTURE

Armstrong sees his future as full of possibilities, but, as with all individuals in their later years, some are more possible than others. He continues to be an inspiration for budding engineers, young scientists, and pilots, as well as for NASA staff around the world. His support for NASA's programs remains unwavering, and he agreed to accompany President George W. Bush and fellow former astronaut John Glenn to Houston for a memorial ceremony on February 4, 2003, for the space shuttle *Columbia* astronauts. Neither he nor Glenn made any public comments during the ceremony.

Armstrong continues to see himself as part of the community of engineers, but he does not wish to be continually singled out within the engineering community merely because he was an astronaut. Although that part of his life remains in the public eye, he has retreated from the spotlight so he can move on and pursue his other interests.

THE CONTINUING IMPORTANCE OF NEIL ARMSTRONG

Part of Armstrong's continuing importance lies in small contributions, such as attending the *Columbia's* memorial ceremony. Part of it also lies in his private nature. His appearances at public events, which may be accompanied by his soft-spoken comments and his wry and unexpected humor, are all the more treasured because of their infrequency.

Additionally, part of Armstrong's continuing importance lies in the perspective he gives concerning the space program's achievements. When he speaks at a conference or an anniversary ceremony, Armstrong repeatedly strives to remind listeners that they should not allow his individual achievements as part of NASA's manned space program to overshadow the contributions of the hundreds of thousands of Americans who contributed to the effort; he was just part of a much larger team. He also reminds his audience that, to him, being the first to walk on the Moon was not as significant an engineering achievement as was landing on the Moon, which he points out was something that he and Buzz Aldrin accomplished together.

Regardless of whether or not Armstrong is remembered as part of a larger team, his place in history as the first person to set foot on the Moon is secure. Other astronauts and individuals from the early days of NASA have written memoirs of their experiences, and some wish that Armstrong would do likewise. However, he may never do so, and it would be completely in keeping with his character. The self-proclaimed "nerdy engineer" is comfortable with who he is, what he has done in his life, and how he has led it—quietly and privately, but with a great impact on the history of humankind.

Notes

Introduction: Apollo 11, *July 20, 1969*

1. Quoted in John Noble Wilford, *We Reach the Moon: The* New York Times *Story of Man's Greatest Adventure.* New York: Bantam, 1969, p. 267.

2. Quoted in John Barbour and the writers and editors of the Associated Press, *Footprints on the Moon.* New York: American Book—Stratford Press, 1969, p. 208.

3. Quoted in Barbour and others, *Footprints on the Moon,* p. 210.

4. Quoted in Michael Collins, *Carrying the Fire: An Astronaut's Journeys.* New York: Farrar, Straus and Giroux, 1989, p. 451.

Chapter 1: Dreams of Flight

5. Wilford, *We Reach the Moon,* p. 241.

6. Quoted in Wilford, *We Reach the Moon,* p. 241.

7. Quoted in Gene Farmer and Dora Jane Hamblin, *First on the Moon: A Voyage with Neil Armstrong, Michael Collins, and Edwin E. Aldrin, Jr.* Boston: Little, Brown, 1970, p. 12.

8. Quoted in "Gemini Astronauts David R. Scott—Neil A. Armstrong," *New York Times,* March 17, 1966, p. 20.

9. Quoted in Farmer and Hamblin, *First on the Moon,* p. 114.

10. Neil A. Armstrong, "NASA Oral History Transcript," Johnson Space Center Oral History Project, interview by Stephen E. Ambrose and Douglas Brinkley, September 19, 2001, p. 4. www.jsc.nasa.gov.

11. Armstrong, "NASA Oral History," p. 7.

12. Farmer and Hamblin, *First on the Moon,* p. 115.

Chapter 2: The Flying Midshipman

13. Armstrong, "NASA Oral History," p. 13.

14. Quoted in Farmer and Hamblin, *First on the Moon,* p. 115.

15. Armstrong, "NASA Oral History," p. 23.

16. Armstrong, "NASA Oral History," p. 27.

17. Quoted in Farmer and Hamblin, *First on the Moon,* p. 116.

18. Quoted in Farmer and Hamblin, *First on the Moon,* p. 116.

Chapter 3: Challenges in the Air and on the Ground

19. Andrew Chaikin, *A Man on the Moon.* New York: Penguin, 1994, pp. 160–61.

20. Armstrong, "NASA Oral History," p. 36.

21. Chaikin, *A Man on the Moon,* p. 162.

22. Armstrong, "NASA Oral History," p. 33.

23. Armstrong, "NASA Oral History," p. 33.

24. Armstrong, "NASA Oral History," p. 33.

25. Loyd S. Swenson Jr. et al., *This New Ocean: A History of Project Mercury,* NASA History Series, no. 4201. www.hq.nasa.gov.

26. Chaikin, *A Man on the Moon,* p. 163.

Chapter 4: Dreams of Flying in Space

27. Quoted in Barbour and others, *Footprints on the Moon,* p. 15.

28. Neil Armstrong, "I Decided to Get Aboard," in "The Men Write About Themselves and What They Are Up to Now," *Life,* September 27, 1963, p. 84.

29. Armstrong, "NASA Oral History," p. 52.

30. Armstrong, "NASA Oral History," p. 48.

31. Quoted in Chaikin, *A Man on the Moon,* p. 168.

32. Quoted in Chaikin, *A Man on the Moon,* p. 51.

Chapter 5: Dreams of the Moon

33. Donald K. Slayton with Michael Cassutt, *Deke!* New York: Forge/Tom Doherty Associates, 1994, p. 120.

34. Quoted in Slayton with Cassutt, *Deke!* p. 189.

35. Armstrong, pp. 59–60.

36. Buzz Aldrin and Malcolm McConnell, *Men from Earth.* New York: Bantam, 1989, p. 187.

37. D.C. Agle, "We Called It 'the Bug,'" *Air & Space,* August–September 2001, p. 68.

38. Slayton with Cassut, *Deke!* p. 223.

39. Slayton with Cassutt, *Deke!* p. 224.

Chapter 6: Training for the Moon

40. Armstrong, "NASA Oral History," p. 65.

41. Armstrong, "NASA Oral History," p. 73.

42. Armstrong, "NASA Oral History," p. 79.

43. Aldrin and McConnell, p. 215.

44. Quoted in Farmer and Hamblin, *First on the Moon,* p. 27.

45. Quoted in Farmer and Hamblin, *First on the Moon,* p. 209.

Chapter 7: A Dream Come True

46. Quoted in Farmer and Hamblin, *First on the Moon,* p. 31.

47. Quoted in Farmer and Hamblin, *First on the Moon,* p. 70.

48. Quoted in Farmer and Hamblin, *First on the Moon,* p. 231.

49. Chaikin, *A Man on the Moon,* pp. 194–95.

50. Quoted in Farmer and Hamblin, *First on the Moon,* p. 246.

51. Chaikin, *A Man on the Moon,* p. 200.

52. Armstrong, "NASA Oral History," p. 84.

53. Quoted in Farmer and Hamblin, *First on the Moon,* p. 267.

54. Quoted in Farmer and Hamblin, *First on the Moon,* p. 268.

55. Quoted in Chaikin, *A Man on the Moon,* p. 211.

56. John F. Kennedy Space Center, "Apollo 11," February 21, 2003. http://www-pao.ksc.nasa.gov.

57. Armstrong, "NASA Oral History," p. 85.

58. Quoted in Farmer and Hamblin, *First on the Moon,* p. 312.

59. Quoted in Farmer and Hamblin, *First on the Moon,* p. 329.

60. Quoted in Associated Press, "Apollo Wives Are Terribly Proud," *New York Times,* July 25, 1969, p. 31.

61. Collins, *Carrying the Fire,* p. 452.

Chapter 8: Retreating from the Spotlight

62. Armstrong, "NASA Oral History," p. 89.

63. Chaikin, *A Man on the Moon,* p. 568.

64. Quoted in R. Sherrod, "Interview with Neil Alden Armstrong, Office Building 10B, NASA Hq., 23 September, 1971 with RS," http://history.nasa.gov, p. 2.

65. Kathy Sawyer, "The Quiet Man on the Moon: Neil Armstrong's Code: Solitary, Self-Sufficient and Mostly Silent," *Florida Today Space Online,* July 18, 1999. www.floridatoday.com.

66. Armstrong, "NASA Oral History," p. 90.

67. Quoted in Chaikin, *A Man on the Moon,* p. 569.

68. Quoted in Sawyer, "The Quiet Man on the Moon," p. 9.

69. Armstrong, "NASA Oral History," p. 92.

70. Paul Hoversten, "Neil Armstrong: Self-Proclaimed 'Nerdy Engineer,'" Space.com, February 23, 2000. www.space.com.

71. Armstrong, "NASA Oral History," p. 88.

72. Hoversten, "Neil Armstrong."

73. Quoted in Marcia Dunn, "Neil Armstrong, 30 Years Later: Still Reticent After All These Years," July 14, 1999. http://abcnews.go.com.

For Further Reading

Books

John Barbour and the writers and editors of the Associated Press, *Footprints on the Moon*. New York: American Book—Stratford Press, Inc., 1969. This book covers the early history of the U.S. space program, from the days of *Sputnik* to *Apollo 11*.

Carmen Bredeson, *Neil Armstrong: A Space Biography* (Countdown to Space Series). Berkeley Heights, NJ: Enslow, 1998. Beginning with *Apollo 11*'s flight, this biography covers the period before and after Armstrong's accomplishments with NASA.

Robert Godwin, ed., *Apollo 11: The NASA Mission Reports.* Vol. 3. Burlington, ON, Canada: Apogee, 2002. Full of technical information, this book contains diagrams showing the descent of the lunar module, photos of the lunar surface, medical observations about the human body on the Moon, and a DVD with footage from the *Eagle* descending from lunar orbit and the astronauts' Moon walk.

Barbara Kramer, *Neil Armstrong: The First Man on the Moon* (People to Know series). Berkeley Heights, NJ: Enslow, 1997. This book documents not only Armstrong's public achievements but some of the aspects of his private life as well.

Stephanie Maze, *I Want to Be an Astronaut.* Orlando, FL: Harcourt, 1999. This book explains what it is like to be an astronaut, from the history of the manned space program and educational requirements to areas of specialization within the profession.

David Reynolds, with Wally Schirra and Von Hardesty, *Apollo: The Epic Journey to the Moon.* Orlando, FL: Harcourt, 2002. The numerous photos and drawings help illustrate the concepts of the entire Apollo program.

Paul Westman, *Neil Armstrong: Space Pioneer.* Minneapolis: Lerner, 1980. Designed for younger readers, this book covers the highlights of Armstrong's contributions to the space program.

Periodicals

The weekly *Life* magazine had an exclusive arrangement with NASA to provide its readers with biographies of the astronauts and glimpses into their training regimens and their family lives. Neil Armstrong is introduced to *Life*'s readers in the September 30, 1963, issue, which includes the backgrounds of Armstrong and the other astronauts of the "New Nine." The crisis during the *Gemini VIII* flight is covered in the March 25, 1966, edition. The *Apollo 11* flight is covered in the issues of July and August 1969.

Countless newspapers across the United States and around the world covered the events of the manned space program. Some of the best coverage was provided by the *New York Times;* the newspaper's banner headline for July 21, 1969, said simply, "Men Walk on Moon."

Videotapes

From the Earth to the Moon, HBO Films, 1998. Based in part on Andrew Chaikin's book *A Man on the Moon*, this miniseries examines the U.S. space program from President Kennedy's 1961 challenge to the final *Apollo* flight in 1973, concentrating on the men and women who made it happen.

NASA 25 Years, Madacy Entertainment Group, Inc. (P.O. Box 1445, St-Laurent, QC H4L 4Z1 Canada). Twenty original NASA films compiled into a boxed set. *This Is Houston Flight* deals with the flight and emergency procedures related to the recovery of *Gemini 8. The Eagle Has Landed* covers the flight of *Apollo 11.*

To the Moon, WGBH Boston. Part of the award-winning series NOVA, this film takes a look at the Apollo program. Rare footage and interviews with astronauts and other NASA personnel highlight this two-hour film.

Internet Sources

The Neil Armstrong Air & Space Museum's website (www.ohiohistory.org) gives information about the Wapakoneta, Ohio, museum that helps keep Armstrong's legacy alive.

NASA's website (nasa.gov) has a tremendous amount of resource material available. Many important documents associated with the early days of the space program, such as the *Apollo 1* disaster report, are available online. In addition, NASA's "The Space Educators' Handbook," located at vesuvius.jsc.nasa.gov./er/seh/seh.html title contains a vast amount of grade-specific material for educators, including sections titled "Space Math," "Space Robotics," and "Space Cool Stuff."

Works Consulted

Books

Buzz Aldrin and Malcolm McConnell, *Men from Earth*. New York: Bantam, 1989. Aldrin presents a frank and revealing look at NASA's space program and the demands it put on its employees, as well as his personal problems in the years after he left NASA.

Frank Borman with Robert J. Sterling, *Countdown: An Autobiography*. New York: Silver Arrow/William Morrow, 1988. Borman shares his observations on the manned space program, including his role in the *Apollo 1* investigation and his command of *Apollo 8*.

Andrew Chaikin, *A Man on the Moon*. New York: Penguin, 1994. A basis for the HBO miniseries *From the Earth to the Moon*, this is a highly informative and readable history of the Gemini and Apollo programs, presented through the eyes of its participants.

Michael Collins, *Carrying the Fire: An Astronaut's Journeys*. New York: Farrar, Straus and Giroux, 1989. This book presents a more personal look at the manned space program than many others.

Gene Farmer and Dora Jane Hamblin, *First on the Moon: A Voyage with Neil Armstrong, Michael Collins, and Edwin E. Aldrin, Jr.* Boston: Little, Brown, 1970. *Life* magazine writers Farmer and Hamblin draw on their interviews with Armstrong, Aldrin, and Collins in presenting a detailed account of the *Apollo 11* voyage.

Barton C. Hacker and James M. Grimwood, *On the Shoulders of Titans: A History of Project Gemini*. Houston: NASA Special Publications Series, 1977. This massively detailed work documents the challenges and achievements of the Gemini program, with particular emphasis on the development of new technologies.

Richard S. Lewis, *The Voyages of Apollo: The Exploration of the Moon*. New York: Quadrangle/*New York Times* Book, 1974. A comprehensive look at the Apollo program, with interviews.

Jim Lovell and Jeffrey Kluger, *Lost Moon: The Perilous Voyage of Apollo 13*. Boston: Houghton Mifflin, 1994. Lovell examines his role in the space program, including his Gemini and Apollo flights before his command of the *Apollo 13* mission.

Alan Shepard and Deke Slayton, with Jay Barbree and Howard Benedict, *Moon Shot: The Inside Story of America's Race to the Moon*. Atlanta: Turner, 1994. Slayton and Shepard, who at one time ran the Astronaut Office at NASA, share their views of the U.S. side of the space race.

Donald K. Slayton with Michael Cassutt, *Deke!* New York: Forge/Tom Doherty Associates, 1994. Slayton, one of the Mercury astronauts, shares his story, touching on issues such as his years before and after NASA and his battle with cancer.

John Noble Wilford, *We Reach the Moon: The New York Times Story of Man's Greatest Adventure.* New York: Bantam, 1969. *New York Times* reporter Wilford was an eyewitness to the development of the manned space program and recounts the *Apollo 11* mission based on his reports from Cape Kennedy and Houston.

Periodicals

D.C. Agle, "We Called It 'the Bug,'" *Air & Space,* August–September 2001.

Neil Armstrong, "I Decided to Get Aboard," in "The Men Write About Themselves and What They Are Up to Now," in *Life,* September 27, 1963.

Associated Press, "Apollo Wives Are 'Terribly Proud,'" *New York Times,* July 25, 1969.

Associated Press, "Armstrong Museum Urged," *New York Times,* July 22, 1969.

Joseph Bourque, "Shooting the Moon: How a Clever Camera and Its Irascible Inventor Captured the Lunar Surface—but Not the Hearts of Apollo Astronauts," *Air & Space,* April–May 2002.

Bernard Gwertzman, "Luna Mission Ends; Soviet Craft Down on Moon—Tass Says Work Is Finished," *New York Times,* July 22, 1969.

Bernard Gwertzman, "Soviet Launches Unmanned Craft Towards the Moon," *New York Times,* July 14, 1969.

Dan Kovalchik, "The Rocket Ships: Tracking Launches from Cape Canaveral Required Old Boats and Iron Guts," *Air & Space,* December 2001–January 2002.

George Leopold, "Neil Armstrong, Presenting Century's Top Tech Feats, Cites Engineering's Contributions to 'Human Happiness'—First Engineer on the Moon Lauds Colleagues' Leaps," *Electronic Engineering Times,* February 28, 2000.

Life, "The Astronauts—Their Own Great Stories," August 22, 1969.

Life, "'Come On Trolley!': Photos Capture the Apollo Astronauts' Families As They Watch Moon Landing," August 1, 1969.

Life, "High Tension over the Astronauts," March 25, 1966.

Life, "Three Men Bound for the Moon," July 4, 1969.

Richard D. Lyons, "NASA Officials Fear Russians Are Trying to Upstage Apollo," *New York Times,* July 14, 1969.

New York Times. "Gemini Astronauts David R. Scott—Neil A. Armstrong," March 17, 1966.

Matthew Purdy, "In Rural Ohio, Armstrong Quietly Lives on Own Dark Side of the Moon," *New York Times,* July 20, 1994.

Patrick T. Reardon, "A Quiet Hero Speaks: Neil Armstrong Finally Opens Up—a Little Bit," *Chicago Tribune,* October 2, 2002.

Walter Rugaber, "Nixon Makes 'Most Historic Telephone Call Ever,'" *New York Times,* July 21, 1969.

Walter Rugaber, "Parades and a Reception Set in 3 Cities on Aug. 13," *New York Times,* July 23, 1969.

Harold M. Schmeck Jr., "Crew That Will Join Astronauts in Quarantine Already

Living in Isolation," *New York Times,* July 23, 1969.

Harold M. Schmeck Jr., "Two Men Adjust Quickly to Conditions on Moon," *New York Times,* July 21, 1969.

Les Schneider, "The Homecoming," *American Heritage,* December 1992.

William K. Stevens, "The Crew: What Kind of Men Are They?" *New York Times,* July 17, 1969.

United Press International, "Only One Apollo Wife to See the Launching," *New York Times,* July 16, 1969.

John Noble Wilford, "Apollo Astronauts Are 'Willing and Ready,'" *New York Times,* July 15, 1969.

John Noble Wilford, "Apollo Crew Takes Break and Countdown Resumes," *New York Times,* July 14, 1969.

John Noble Wilford, *"Gemini 8* Crew Is Forced down in Pacific After Successful Linkup with Satellite; Spacemen Picked up After 3 Hours in Sea," *New York Times,* March 17, 1966.

John Noble Wilford, "Million at Cape; Countdown Goes 'Well' for Launching of Eight-Day Voyage," *New York Times,* July 16, 1969.

John Noble Wilford, "A Powdery Surface Is Closely Examined," *New York Times,* July 21, 1969.

Richard Witkin, "Borman Assails Nixon Dinner Ban," *New York Times,* July 13, 1969.

Richard Witkin, "Shortly Before Landing, Armstrong Took Over from Computer," *New York Times,* July 21, 1969.

James T. Wooten, "Recovery Team in Pacific Ends Final Rehearsal; 'We're All Set,' Chief Says," *New York Times,* July 22, 1969.

Internet Sources

Neil A. Armstrong, "NASA Johnson Space Center Oral History Project: Oral History Transcript," interview Stephen E. Armstrong and Douglas Brinkley, September 19, 2001. www.jsc.nasa.gov.

Associated Press, "One Small Step for a Man? Even Armstrong Isn't Sure It's 'A' or Nay," July 18, 1999. www.flatoday.com.

BBC News, "Frustration on Moonwalk Anniversary," July 20, 1999. BBC Online Network, http://news.bbc.co.uk.

Courtney G. Brooks and Ivan D. Ertel, "The Apollo Spacecraft—A Chronology, Volume III, Part 1 (E): Advanced Design, Fabrication, and Testing, February 1965," n.d. www.hq.nasa.gov.

Courtney G. Brooks and Ivan D. Ertel, National Aeronautics and Space Administration, "The Apollo Spacecraft—A Chronology, Volume III, Part 1 (F): Advanced Design, Fabrication, and Testing, March 1965," n.d. www.hq.nasa.gov.

Department of the Navy, Naval Historical Center, "United Nations and Republic of Korea Forces—Overview and Special Image Selection," September 10, 2000. www.history.navy.mil.

Jim Dumoulin, NASA-Kennedy Space Center, "Project Gemini," August 25, 2000. http://science.ksc.nasa.gov.

Marcia Dunn, "Neil Armstrong, 30 years Later: Still Reticent After All These

Years," July 14, 1999. http://abcnews.go.com.

Lee Dye, "Neil and Buzz an Unlikely Duo," ABCNEWS.com.http://abcnews.go.com.

EDO Corporation, "EDO Corporation CEO James M. Smith to Become Chairman upon Retirement of Neil Armstrong," February 8, 2002. www.edocorp.com.

EDO Corporation, "Executive Profile," 2000. www.nycedo.com.

Ivan D. Ertel and Roland W. Newkirk, National Aeronautics and Space Administration, "The Apollo Spacecraft—A Chronology, Volume IV, Part 1 (F): Preparation for Flight, the Accident, and Investigation, February 1967," n.d. www.hq.nasa.gov.

Ivan D. Ertel and Roland W. Newkirk, National Aeronautics and Space Administration, "The Apollo Spacecraft—A Chronology, Volume IV Part 1 (G): Preparation for Flight, the Accident, and Investigation, March 1 through March 16, 1967," n.d. www.hq.nasa.gov.

Ivan D. Ertel and Roland W. Newkirk, National Aeronautics and Space Administration, "The Apollo Spacecraft—A Chronology, Volume IV, Part 1 (H): Preparation for Flight, the Accident, and Investigation, March 16 through April 5, 1967," n.d. www.hq.nasa.gov.

Ivan D. Ertel and Roland W. Newkirk, National Aeronautics and Space Administration, "The Apollo Spacecraft—A Chronology, Volume IV, Part 2 (G): Recovery, Spacecraft Redefinition, and First Manned Apollo Flight, December 1967," n.d. www.hq.nasa.gov.

Ivan D. Ertel and Roland W. Newkirk, National Aeronautics and Space Administration, "The Apollo Spacecraft—A Chronology, Appendix 7: Funding," n.d. www.hq.nasa.gov.

Flying Midshipmen Association, "Museum Matters: Aviation Midshipmen Display," n.d. www.flyingmidshipmen.org.

Amy E. Foster, "Aeronautical Science 101: The Development of Engineering Science in Aeronautical Engineering at the University of Minnesota," 1999. www.aem.umn.edu.

Paul Hoversten, "Neil Armstrong: Self-Proclaimed 'Nerdy Engineer,'" Space.com, February 23, 2000. www.space.com.

John F. Kennedy Space Center, *Apollo 11,* February 21, 2003. www-pao.ksc.nasa.gov.

Eric M. Jones, National Aeronautics and Space Administration, "Lunar Surface Journal: The First Lunar Landing," December 28, 2002. www.hq.nasa.gov.

Angela M. Kneller, "Auglaize County, Ohio," November 10, 2002. www.kneller.com.

National Aeronautics and Space Administration, "The Apollo Spacecraft—A Chronology," n.d. www.hq.nasa.gov.

James Oberg, "Uncovering Soviet Disasters: Chapter 10: Dead Cosmonauts," 1998. www.fas.org.

Ohio Historical Society, "Neil Armstrong Air & Space Museum," December 18, 2002. www.ohiohistory.org.

Kathy Sawyer, "The Quiet Man on the Moon: Neil Armstrong's Code: Solitary, Self-Sufficient and Mostly Silent," *Florida Today Space Online,* July 18, 1999. www.floridatoday.com.

R. Sherrod, "Interview with Neil Alden Armstrong, Office Building 10B, NASA Hq., 23 September 1971 with RS." http.//history.nasa.gov.

State of Ohio Department of Development, Office of Strategic Research, "Ohio County Profiles: Auglaize County," n.d. www.odod.state.oh.us.

Loyd S. Swenson Jr. et al., 1989. *This New Ocean: A History of Project Mercury.* NASA History Series, no. 4201. www.hq. nasa.gov.

University of Minnesota, "History of the Aeronautical Engineering Department of the University of Minnesota 1929–1962." www.aem.umn.edu.

Jerry Woodfill, National Aeronautics and Space Administration, "Space Educators' Handbook," December 11, 2002. http://vesuvius.jsc.nasa.gov.

Deborah Zabarenko, "U.S. Marks Wright Centennial As Aviation Struggles," Reuters, December 17, 2002. http://story. news.yahoo.com.

Index

lunar module
  building of, 52
  landing of, on moon,
    10–11, 77–82
  pilot backup and, 60
  simulator of, 58, 61, 62,
    70–72
Lunar Receiving
  Laboratory (LRL), 82,
  83

Mach, speed of sound
  and, 34
Man on the Moon, A
  (Chaikin), 55
Manned Space Center
  (Houston, Texas), 43,
  46, 52, 83
Mars, opinion about
  mission to, 90
McDivitt, Jim, 38, 45, 58,
  59, 63
McDonnell Douglas
  Aircraft factory (St.
  Louis, Missouri), 46
Mercury (NASA
  program), 37–39, 40
Mercury Seven, 40, 43,
  45
midshipman, flying, 24
Mission Control, 49, 70
missions, manned. *See*
  space flight, manned
moon
  Apollo 11's mission to,
    10–11, 73–83
  goal of landing on, 40,
    46, 47, 52–61
  landing on, 77–82

no atmosphere on, 81
reduced gravity of, 55
rocks of, 80
Sea of Tranquility on,
  68, 78
speed and position of,
  66–67
surface of, 11, 80
training for mission to,
  62–72
Music out of the Moon
  (recording) (Hoffman),
  81

NACA. *See* National
  Advisory Council for
  Aeronautics
NASA
  Apollo program and,
    39, 44, 52–83
  first manned orbit and,
    37
  Gemini program and,
    39, 40, 42–43, 44–52
  investigation of
    procedures and, 54
  John F. Kennedy and,
    40
  Johnson Space Center
    Oral History Project
    and, 14, 90, 92
  language of, 64
  Mercury program and,
    37–39, 40
  mission of, 33
  press conference and, 73
National Advisory
  Council for
  Aeronautics (NACA),
  26–28

High Speed Flight
  Station, 29–32
renamed NASA, 33
National Aeronautics
  and Space
  Administration. *See*
  NASA
Naval Reserve Officer
  Training Corps
  (NROTC), 18–20, 24
navy. *See* U.S. Navy
Neifer, Earl K., 25
Neil Armstrong Air and
  Space Museum, 89
New Nine, 38–39, 40–41,
  45
1950s, developing
  aircraft designs
  during, 31
Nixon, Richard M.
  on *Apollo 11*'s mission,
    11
  greeted returning
    astronauts, 83, 84
  signed plaque that
    remained on moon,
    80–81
North American
  Aviation
  analysis of designs for,
    54
  builder of command
    modules for, 52

Ohio, childhood life in,
  12–17
On the Shoulders of Titans
  (Hacker and
  Grimwood), 50

Tranquility Base, on moon, 78, 80
tumbling, out of control, 49
Turner, Roscoe, 14

University of Cincinnati, 86–87
U.S. Air Force, 30
U.S. Navy
  required Armstrong's active duty, 22–26
  scholarship program of, 18–19
USS *Essex* (aircraft carrier), 24, 25, 26
USS *Hornet* (aircraft carrier), 83
USSR. *See* Soviet Union

veterans
  GI bill and, 20
  World War II, 26
VF-51 aircraft fighter squadron, 24, 25
Vietnam War, 19
Voskhod 2 (Soviet space capsule), *45*
Vostok 3 (Soviet space capsule), *44*
Vostok 4 (Soviet space capsule), *44*

Wapakoneta, Ohio, 12, 15–17, 27, 89
weightlessness
  in space, 40
  training for, 46
White, Ed, 38, 43, 44, 45

death of, 52–55
White, Pat, 43, 44, 55
wind tunnel, young Armstrong builds, 15, 22
Wise, Joseph, 22
wives, of astronauts, 55
World War II, 17, 20, 23, 24
Wright brothers, 14

X-1 (airplane), 20
X-15 (airplane), 30, 33–39
"X projects," 29–30

Yeager, Charles E., 20–22
Young, John, 38, 45, 63

Zwez, John, 89

Picture Credits

Cover: © Bettmann/CORBIS

© Bettmann/CORBIS, 13, 27, 41,
    48, 56, 60, 70, 74, 79

© CORBIS Sygma, 65

COREL Corporation, 69, 71

Getty Images, 91

Chris Jouan, 47, 59, 63, 75, 86

Library of Congress, 23

NASA, 10, 17, 30, 31, 35, 37,
    42, 43, 50, 53, 57, 77 (both),
    80, 85, 88

© Smithsonian Institution, 15

Time Life Pictures, 67

USAF Photo Museum Archives, 21

About the Author

As a youngster, Andrew A. Kling was fascinated with the stars, the planets, and the space race. On July 20, 1969, he listened with awe to the *Apollo 11* Moon landing on the radio of his family's VW bus as they were traveling in Wales. He has followed the space programs of the world ever since.

After more than fifteen years with the National Park Service, he now lives in Montana, working as a freelance writer and media development consultant.